TOLD

Messages from a Greater Conscious or the Ramblings of a Madman

JOHN SEER

The Choir Press

Copyright © 2025 John Seer

All rights reserved. No part of this publication may be reproduced or transmitted in any form or by any means, electronic or mechanical including photocopying, recording or any information storage or retrieval system, without prior permission in writing from the publishers.

The right of John Seer to be identified as the author of this work has been asserted by him in accordance with the Copyright, Designs and Patents Act 1988

First published in the United Kingdom in 2025 by
The Choir Press

ISBN 978-1-78963-517-1

Contents

Introduction	v
Star (A poem for the 21st century)	ix
Final note	xv

Chapter 1	The Blow to the Head	1
Chapter 2	The Close Encounter	4
Chapter 3	The Monk on the Train	7
Chapter 4	When someone we love Dies	15
Chapter 5	The Will to be vs the Will to not be	19
Chapter 6	The Greys	25
Chapter 7	UFOs (UAPs)	29
Chapter 8	Natural Wi-Fi	31
Chapter 9	Our Elders and Saviours	37
Chapter 10	AI to AGI to Advanced AI	41
Chapter 11	The Drive to Support the Spiritual Way	45
Chapter 12	The Soulless Elite	50
Chapter 13	The Meaning of Life	58
Chapter 14	The Great Destruction	61
Chapter 15	Jesus Christ (Isa)	65
Chapter 16	God's Little Hacks	71
Chapter 17	Who is Really to Blame	73
Chapter 18	Not So Common, Common Sense	75
Chapter 19	The Current Emergency and the Greys	78
Chapter 20	The Presence of the Soul	81

Chapter 21 Ghosts	83
Chapter 22 Spiritual vs Material	88
Chapter 23 Who We Really Are	91
Chapter 24 Conspiracy investigators	94
Chapter 25 Immortality the Only Reality	96
Chapter 26 The Satan	97
Chapter 27 The Apocalypse	102
Chapter 28 Armageddon	105
Chapter 29 AI like Jesus or AI like Satan	109
Chapter 30 The Second Coming	113

Introduction

The first thought you had was probably a question.
The last thought you will have will probably be a question.
We spend our lives asking questions.
But we never really get the answers to the questions that really matter.
We get manmade answers to manmade questions every day, answered by some 'educated' person, or through a search engine on the internet, or in a book, that help us with our day-to-day living, superficial answers to superficial questions, but answers to deeper questions rarely get answered, and even more rarely get answered correctly.
So it feels quite significant to get answers that resonate so strongly as true to the deeper, usually unanswered questions.
It's strange, but most times we know an answer is true because we find ourselves thinking, that's it! I knew that! As if the answer was already in there, we just needed reminding. That is because it often is.
As in the right state, our conscious mind can naturally dip into a pool of knowledge I like to call the Greater Conscious that silently drip feeds information to us.
So when we hear the truth, often we realise we already knew it.
I am not capable of writing a book like this. I have found it as interesting to read as anyone else who reads it.
Sometimes I'm reading it as I'm writing it.
I even say 'wow' sometimes, as I write something down, that answers a question I had longed to know the answer to.
Now I understand more about life, I am now very happy to have been poorly educated in the traditional way. I don't see it as a weakness anymore, I see it as a lucky escape.
Education often seems to find itself looking up to and studying people that were actually uneducated, and I believe the reason these uneducated people became worthy of studying was because they had to rely on intuition, and were not filled with other people's recycled and often faulty ideas.
The most highly academic people have such powerful physical

memory banks, and such powerful physical calculators, that their barking dog ego brains are so loud they have virtually no chance at all of being able to connect to the Greater Conscious through their minds.

This is why you find that many intellectuals are unable to understand or accept spirituality or God. It takes someone with an incredibly powerful spirit, or in other words a powerful connection to the Greater Conscious, to override a loud intellectual brain.

Very few people have both and can be considered a true genius if they do.

Who knows whether these drips and sparks of images and information that pop in my head from somewhere, are really from the Greater Conscious as I am told, or just crazy ideas from a damaged head, but the one thing I do know is they do make a lot of sense to me, and answer questions most can't answer.

Only time will tell if they are true or not.

This book's contents could be described as hypothesis or theory, but I would have to have put quite a lot of mental effort into imagining or inventing all these things for the contents to be described in that way, and the only mental effort on my part was trying to put subjects in the right order, and trying to translate the thoughts and images into a clear and concise manner, so people can understand what I think I'm supposed to convey.

I feel like a human pen being used to write out things that are beyond me, but as it is coming through me, it is getting simplified so everyone can understand it.

As I understand it, if a subject, however complicated, is not explainable in simple terms, it's either not being explained properly or it's wrong.

I believe receiving information like this is happening to a lot of people in different ways, especially at this most crucial time in our history.

I'm writing these experiences down as I feel a constant pressure to do so that increases monthly now.

The pressure to write it feels like when you were a kid and your dad put his hand on your back to help you up a hill or when your mum gently but firmly reminded you to do your homework.

So, it's not nasty, it just has a weight to it, like it needs to get done to contribute, and as I say I'm told a lot of others now more than ever are getting tasked in different ways.

Sometimes these happenings are like how you would imagine receiving information telepathically, sometimes it's like remote viewing, sometimes it's an image, and sometimes I'm actually there but sometimes even more than that, sometimes I'm also given the emotions and the essence of the happening itself.

There is only one truth about everything, and it's all from the same pool, the Greater Conscious, so parts of this information will be similar, or even the same as information from others, it has to be, because it's true, and has come from the same pool that they have also dipped into.

The more people that draw from the pool the better, sometimes reinforcing the truth by saying the same or similar things, and sometimes getting closer to the full truth by introducing new things, but eventually we will put all the pieces together and realise the whole picture.

The intention of this book is to bring people's conscious attention to the information it contains, as everything is made of consciousness. Raising attention to an idea or potential happening can change things in the places we cannot see, then in turn can change things in the places we can see, in a similar way to how one would manifest a situation.

You would be amazed how powerful your thoughts can be.

They really can alter an outcome, as consciousness and so conscious thought is the only thing that is real. The one thing we think is not real turns out to be the only thing that really is.

I use the analogy of a pool or an ocean quite often because it seems a lot of nonphysical things are best explained in this form.

The pool that I receive this information from is in the spiritual dimension, it is an open pool that everyone with a conscious, or if you prefer a soul, can access, so although there may be many things that you haven't heard before there will be some things that you have, albeit maybe in a different way, as the truth is the truth.

I only really listen to the Greater Conscious now, as I don't see the point in getting information from second-hand or imaginative sources. But I do sometimes (in between writing) listen to people I like and respect on the internet which sometimes lights up a question for me to ask, that I get an answer to later, or nudges a memory of information I had forgotten.

The more I've dipped into the pool, the more a correct answer from another person rings true, or close to true in a strange way.

What is constantly happening to me every day is questions being answered in part like the edges of a jigsaw and then slowly over days or weeks the centre gets filled in.

It gets slowly dripped in, as it's not my mind that could not take it, as the mind is infinite. It's the final destination of the information, which is my physical brain, that could not take too much at once.

Sending too much at once would be like a nuclear power station sending a full load to an AA battery.

There is a field around us in the physical dimension as well that allows our conscious thoughts to pass to one another, it's best known as the Ether.

It is only possible for an individual to connect to the Ether if they are able to connect to the Greater Conscious. As although they are two completely different things, the system used is the same. In other words, if the individual's brain can be silenced enough to enable their brain to realise information sent through the conscious mind from the Greater Conscious, they are also able to connect to information from the Ether, as the mind can connect to the Ether as well as the Greater Conscious, and so pass information onto the brain. Albeit the Greater Conscious is in the spiritual dimension and the Ether sits within the very inner workings of the physical dimension.

Whenever someone consciously acknowledges something true, that thought then goes out to the Ether, or should I say goes within.

The Ether is a frequency in this physical dimension and is within what some people call the quantum realm.

That thought is then highlighted in some way to other consciousnesses, and it seems it is then a helping hand for them to get the information themselves from the Greater Conscious. It's like a sign or a tag on something true and of importance. So, this is why when someone consciously acknowledges a truth in this dimension, it isn't long before others in that same time period also start realising it.

I guess this book is a very basic physical version of that.

Anyway, jigsaws keep getting filled all the time. But there has to be a point where you get out what you know, as the pool is infinite.

By the way, that ability of conscious-to-conscious communication within the Ether is the basis of telepathy. It's an ability we once had that some of us are getting back fast. There's never been a more needed time and maybe that's why.

Star

(A poem for the twenty-first century, inspired
by Rudyard Kipling's 'If')

If you can strongly disagree with the opinions of others, but still keep them as your friends.
If you can stand by what you believe, when all around submit.
If you can value courage and free will as your greatest assets.
If you can conquer the fear of ridicule and so break its remote control.
If you can see that debt is slavery and caring what others think are the chains.
If you can judge a person by their actions, not their label, the colour of their spirit and not their skin.
If you can know that everything physical is an illusion and the only real you is the eternal part of you, that you cannot see.
If you can stand up and speak freely, when you know it could cost you dearly.
If you can realise that your thoughts can affect the world you cannot see, and so alter the world you can.
If you can see through the fog of lies and back those who risk everything to bring the light of truth.
If you can value time with your loved ones over any amount of material gain.
If you can realise that when you stop the barking of your overprotective doglike brain, you will hear the wisdom of the Greater Conscious from where we came.
If you can see that the world is being run by a few soulless parasites, that create fear to take our money and stay in control.
If you can realise the way of nature is the path to joy, and the artificial route leads to our destruction.
If you can see, we are now in the most important of times and help others to see the same.
If you can do at least some of these things
and the rest, just wish to God you had.
You are a star my friend.

My favourite memories of my dad were of him working on his cars at the weekend. Seeing his legs in oil-stained overalls sticking out from under a car in his garage.

I think they are my fondest memories because that was where he was happiest, away from his very high-pressure office job. He often used to sing under the car and his favourite song was Little Boxes, which was a song that was in the charts in the early sixties.

I didn't realise why it was his favourite song until I was about the age he was when he used to sing it.

He was a veteran from some of the hardest experiences of the Second World War, so he enjoyed the song as it was basically about how crazy we humans are. He sang it in a jolly carefree but mocking way, which he would have learnt in the war was the only way to deal with crazy times.

The song is called Little Boxes because it's basically about how crazy it is that we all live in little boxes, all the same.

It's true. When we are born, we are put in a box, and then we spend the first part of our lives learning in boxes, only to spend most of the rest of our lives working in boxes.

We drive inside boxes to get from box to box and walk around inside big boxes to get our food. We spend our evenings watching a box inside a bigger box and then go to sleep in another box. In the end we die and get put in a box.

The song just gets more apt every decade, with more and more boxes. We even have a little box in our pockets now that we can't seem to do without.

Just like the song, little boxes all the same.

The lady that wrote the song and the people like my dad who enjoyed it could obviously see we were on the path of something quite unnatural, probably because they were very unique and individual characters, and the thought of us all being slowly moulded into worker bees, all the same, living in little cells all the same, seemed not only insane but a little scary, especially as systems like this are normally designed for the sole survival of one leader or a small elite group of leaders.

Some people feel that this is happening and spend their lives quietly uncomfortable, and can even appear a little crazy or eccentric, as unfortunately they understand how insane and unnatural this world really is, and they know that the powers that be are not content with just putting us in physical boxes, but also like to divide and conquer by putting us in race boxes, financial status boxes, sexual orientation boxes, etc. etc. and the sad thing is, most other people don't realise any of this, let alone see outside the box.

I have mentioned all this about my dad and boxes, as it was the start of my realisation that we were not living as we should be. Before the song as a young child, my mindset was that the world was sorted, and it was me that needed to sort myself out. After the song I realised that the world had a lot more to sort out than I did.

It was my first tiny crack in the illusionary veil that was hiding the true reality.

One of the ways I receive information is from dreams. So I've picked out two life-changing dreams that happened to me, to give you some idea why my family and I believe this information has substance and is worth telling others. Whether it's from a divine database or not, as it's one thing receiving sensible answers to questions you could never get answers to before, but another when they actually save a life. Then it all gets very real.

I always viewed dreams as nothing more than fantasy when I was younger, as that's what I was taught, and of course some dreams are, but now I know some dreams are a lot more than that.

When I was about thirty-six years old, I dreamt I would get very sick at fifty-six and soon after that I would die. The numbers five and six together were clear and without being too morbid the images of me overweight, drunk and dying were very dark and upsetting. It woke me up and shook me for weeks at the time.

I eventually told my wife, who at the time was just interested in being a hard-working mother and setting up a nice home, with absolutely no interest or belief in anything you couldn't see, apart from once seeing what she thought was a ghost.

Shortly after the dream I stopped smoking and so did my wife to back me up. Then about two years before the age of fifty-six I stopped drinking alcohol purely because of the dream. I clearly should have stopped way before that. Sure enough at fifty-six I became ill and over the next two years a row of serious illnesses threatened my life, culminating in cancer. I'd like to keep this book as upbeat as possible as it's quite heavy at times as it is, so I won't bore you with my illnesses, but the dream was spot on. It was a scary emotional time.

The point I'm getting to is, if I had not had the prior warning from the dream, and so stopped smoking years before, stopped drinking and started taking the steps I did leading up to the age of fifty-six, including putting my knowledge of fasting and natural medicine that I'd learnt because of the dream into practice, I am sure I would not be writing this now.

The push for me to learn about fasting without sugars and with natural medicine was powerful and unremitting.

I think the warning all those years ago, and then my getting ill exactly when it predicted, contributed to my wife taking it more seriously as well, and insisting I do the same, which meant catching it in time to get surgery and have a fighting chance with the natural protocol.

The only other dream I've had that equalled the 'you're gonna die at fifty-six' dream in its vividness, shock and its ability to save a life, was one I had when I was away with my son and sharing a bedroom. I do mention this dream again later as it's perfectly placed there too.

In the dream I was lying on the grass at the top of a hill in a park in London (Greenwich I think) looking over the distant tall towers in the centre of the city. It was uncannily real, the breeze, the people playing, the sounds, tiny vehicles in the distance, warmth from the sun, even freshly cut grass.

Then a bright flash of light from the centre amongst the tall buildings, a wave of smoke ripples out, buildings start falling in its path, heat in my face getting hotter, then a sickeningly loud thudding bang, then I roll into a ditch as the heat and light become so unbearable it woke me up.

As I woke I heard my son choking, I realised he had been sick in his sleep and was choking on his back.

Thankfully I got him on his side quickly so he could breathe and he was ok.

I was double shocked that early morning, and it's never left me. For a long time afterwards, I kept thinking what would have happened if I hadn't been woken up by such a shocking and painful dream. The truth is, he would probably have horribly choked to death, as I'm a very heavy sleeper, especially after drinking red wine.

It also baffled me as I didn't know you could feel pain in a dream.

Anyway, you can see why I believe in some dreams.

I was told shortly afterwards that it was the ideal time to send me that image as although it was showing me a possible future happening that I needed to acknowledge at some time, it was the only dream that would wake me up and so save my son, who also has 'things to do' in his life.

My wife doesn't say much about these things. She's still very much feet on the ground, but when she does, it's quite clear, she now doesn't just have a belief in the supernatural, she knows it.

The book in a nutshell.

Imagine there being a natural internet of knowledge, a spiritual cloud database.

Imagine if you had a personal natural wifi, and that you can sync that wifi with this natural internet and ask it questions.

Imagine then writing a book of the answers you were getting to questions that you could never find answers to before.

Questions you've wondered all your life.

Well, that is what I believe is happening to me, and many others, especially now.

This is an ability most of us have. It's just been forgotten and unused properly for thousands of years, twelve thousand to be precise.

So, it's important to say that none of the stories in this book are my personal opinion, apart from the factual parts that happened to me. These ideas simply pop into my head.

I've tried to explain this in writing so many times, and in so many ways, I'm never really happy with any of my explanations really, but to simply explain it, these emotions, thoughts and images just pop into my head from apparently nowhere, like a download with no effort on my behalf, apart from sometimes asking a question beforehand that was in relation to the answer I later received.

That's the closest way I can explain it.

It's not someone speaking to me. From what I now understand, it is a pool of knowledge I'm dipping into, anyone can dip into it, but when I get the information it still feels like I've been told, so I will say it that way as it's easier.

The information often feels like when someone who is highly qualified in a particular subject tells you something you didn't know, but also often feels like information that down deep you did know but had mostly forgotten, if you see what I mean.

I just happened to get some extra kickstarts to help my personal wifi get going. There were three main situations that did this, I believe, which I will start to explain below and in more detail shortly.

The first one was by a serious head injury to my lower forehead, between my eyes (the area some religious people mark with paint), when I was nine years old and put me in a coma. In that coma I had a near-death experience, in which I went to a place where I felt more at home than I've ever felt before but was sent back and was told I had 'things to do'.

The second was an officially confirmed (then hushed up) UFO encounter by a British warship and two jet fighters in the forces where I received telepathic communication.

Last but definitely not least was a meeting on a night train with a hooded monk, who although I'd never met before was looking around for me in the carriage. A meeting that changed my life, and ended with a literally shocking handshake as I stood to leave the train.

The three things I've mentioned, I believe, have just made it easier for me to sync.

I am no different from anyone else, I've just had some shortcuts to it, and that is all.

So now I get told things. Sometimes I wish I didn't know, and sometimes I'm glad I do. This book is a compilation of notes of what I believe I've been told.

Hopefully if this information is passed through enough consciousness, as everything is made from consciousness, and conscious thought can affect the places we cannot see, and in turn change the things we can see, it may stop this fairy-tale book of fiction becoming a disturbing book of prophecy.

We can always hope.

Final note

I have realised that trying to make all this information have some proper order to it, as one would expect in a book, is impossible and has stopped me finishing this book for twenty or more years, so I've written down what I've been told in the best way I can.

If I've repeated some things, it will be because I felt it was important enough to try different ways to explain it for everyone.

The book won't make any sense if I don't first explain some of the fundamentals and different uses of words from the norm that I have been told and I use in the book.

The mind is not the brain.

Your brain is physical and mortal.

Your mind is spiritual and eternal.

The mind, soul, spirit and conscious are just different words for the same thing.

Your conscious comes from the Greater Conscious.

Another name for the Greater Conscious can be God or heaven.

Another name for the Ether can be the place we cannot see, or the quantum realm.

Anything material or physical is not real.

Only the spirit is real.

Your body is not you.

It is only rented.

More importantly your brain is not you.

Only your spirit (conscious, mind, soul) is you.

It is interesting to me that most of the information I receive is the exact opposite to what we've been taught, even the basic understanding of how everything started is opposite.

I am told consciousness made this physical dimension; it didn't come along afterwards.

So of course, as most things I'm told are the complete opposite of what we think we know, a lot of what I'm told will sound like the ramblings of a mad man.

That's OK, I would not want to seem normal in this upside-down insane asylum.

CHAPTER 1

The Blow to the Head

Strangely, a lot of amazing things can happen to people after a bash on the head.

When I was nine, I had a serious head injury that crushed the front centre of my head, taking a big chip out of my forehead, leaving my eye on my cheek and basically fighting for my life.

I went into a deep coma for days.

I actually did die for a moment but no one ever mentioned that part to me. I was only nine years old so either they didn't want to tell me, or no one knew. I don't know. All I remember is being in a peaceful comforting place of light and then someone I felt very strongly for and wanted to stay with sent me back. It hurt being sent back. 'It's not your time yet,' I felt I heard, 'you have things to do,' and then I woke up.

When I came around the surgeon said that it was literally a miracle that I was alive. It turned out that a fully grown man would have died with that impact, or at least been brain dead. The excellent young surgeon that managed to patch me back together said I had an unusually tough head, which of course my brother interpreted jokingly as unusually thick, as brothers do.

I went home after a few weeks. I'd missed a lot of school, I went back to school eventually to the obvious cruel remarks, as my face was quite disfigured until I healed. Although even when healed it still left a significant indent and scar.

The surgeon seriously warned me to be careful and not to get into any activities that could cause another blow to my head, as the bone in my skull needed to heal and close up a gap that had been caused in the accident.

Of course, after hearing that my imagination ran wild, and I just imagined my soft brain spilling out if I bashed my head. I imagined my skull open with nothing to protect my brain. I became quite paranoid and nervous.

I started life before the accident as a tough little scrapper, and after the accident I became very scared of confrontation and wide open to the bullies, which were many in those days. Right through my early teens I kept imagining my brains would fall out the chip in my head if I got into a fight.

This of course meant as soon as one bully found out that I would not retaliate from physical or verbal abuse, another would have a go. All complete cowards of course.

I remember the day the doctor told me my head was healed, I felt so relieved and so empowered, as he said to me that it was not only healed but had healed thicker than the other side.

I don't know to this day whether he told me that because he knew what paranoia I had about it, or whether it was the truth, but it empowered me anyway.

I immediately joined a boxing club, and funnily enough the bullying stopped straight away, I didn't have to do a thing. But the frustration from those years had built up like a powder keg and boxing only helped a little.

The true damage to my life was that after the accident I didn't really get back into education properly, as I'd missed so much schooling and my brain was also trying to repair. I was put in a low class with people who were not academic and messed about all day, and with teachers that spent the day smoking and dreaming out the window.

I have to say that some of those kids were really bright in a different way. They had incredible common sense and a lot brighter in a real way to the academic kids.

That's where I learnt that, although real intelligence is more important than academic results, in a system that doesn't count common sense you either have to get a trade like most of my mates did in a factory or join the forces.

The country was in recession when I left school. There was little to no work. I didn't even have the qualifications to go to art college. But somehow I managed to get great results down in the army and navy careers office.

A lot of my family going way back were either in the army or the navy, including my dad and grandad, who were highly decorated war heroes, and also both my elder brothers. This added to the pressure of me joining. So reluctantly I also joined.

With regards to the main point of this chapter and being sent back to my life, there was so much to deal with at the time, I didn't really find time to think about it, I just accepted it, as kids do, and dealt with the earthly things.

What was weird was, when it happened, I somehow recognised the entity and knew him very well, felt I'd known him forever and he knew me. The love between us was indescribable, but I didn't click who he was.

A little later in my life I questioned who he was, and although at the time I was not at all impressed with religion or life in general (as the accident had really ruined my life) before my question was finished I knew it was the spirit of Jesus, however embarrassed I had become over the years with even using his name seriously, let alone the whole concept of Jesus.

But that was the answer, and it all clicked into place like truth does.

CHAPTER 2

The Close Encounter

Due to the fact that I signed the armed forces' Official Secrets Act, and was also told by my captain 'What you have just seen, you have not,' I am currently unable to mention the name of the warship involved, or the name of the captain.

Late one evening, early 80s in the seas north of Scotland, a British warship spotted a large stationary object on its radar a few miles off its port bow. It was a very clear night lit by moonlight, and the sea was flat like a mill pond. I was sixteen years old, and part of my duties meant I had to spend time on the bridge of this warship. On entering the bridge, the radio operator and friend of mine pulled me into his curtained side office, and excitedly showed me a big blip on his radar screen and told me to go have a look. I then left the side office and looked out through the bridge front windows. The object was a bright white light, and was sitting about 100 feet from the surface. It was exactly like a bright star. There was no sound coming from the object.

The captain of our warship was called to the bridge. The impression I got was that he reacted in a way that would suggest that this was by no means his first sighting.

The captain then contacted the relevant civilian and military air bases to ask them to confirm any aircraft in the area at the time.

The civilian airbase came back to him with confirmation that there was no civilian aircraft in the area, and then the military airbase came back to him with the same answer, and at that moment the captain asked them for air support. While waiting for the air support to arrive, he had the ship slowly turn towards the light and called for action stations. Which basically means securing the ship for potential conflict. Guns become manned, hatches closed and secured, and everything becomes very serious.

It wasn't very long at all before we saw two jet fighters coming full throttle towards the rear of the ship. I remember looking through the rear starboard door window on the bridge and seeing them coming. It was quite something to see.

The warship was still slowly turning port to point at the object of light. The two fighters roared around the starboard bow of the ship at full throttle and headed towards the object, which was now less than a mile or so away. At this point the ship was almost facing head on, and the object, which hadn't moved at all since I first saw it, suddenly went in a forty-five degree angle so unbelievably fast all you could register in your head was the moisture trail it left in the sky. As soon as this happened one of the pilots spoke on the radio to the warship and the base, saying something along the lines of, 'Jesus Christ, it's gone, it's gone.' The two fighters then circled back around the warship.

As they did this the captain picked the radio back up and said, 'This is Her Majesty's Ship ... Can we confirm an unidentified flying object?' and the answer came back across the radio from the lead pilot, 'We can confirm, I repeat, we can confirm, an unidentified flying object.'

At that point I could hear cheering at the back and sides of the ship from the crew.

When the dust had settled and the crew were back down in the lower deck getting tea and coffee in the dining room, the captain called for the attention of the crew via the on-board intercom saying, 'What you have just seen you have not. Over.'

Nothing ever more was spoken about it out loud, well not on board anyway. The skipper was one of those rare older officers that gained a lot of respect from the lower decks, so if he said don't speak about it, the crew did it's best not to.

The only negative part of this situation was the look on the lads' faces that missed seeing it.

The object, which looked like a star, was white and the shape of an eye, and at a guess, well, put it this way, you could definitely fit a small low house inside it. That sort of size, at a guess between thirty and forty feet wide. It made no sound when it left, certainly none I could hear over the noise of the jet engines and one of the pilots swearing as it left a vapour trail.

The more important part for me, apart from it obviously being probably the most amazing thing I have ever seen, was that something else was going on the whole time.

When I first saw the starlike object, I consciously asked, "What is that?' I immediately got a knowledge in my head of what it was, and who it was. I say knowledge as it was formed in my head rather than explained. So, I got it with no effort, if you see what I mean. It was like an instant package of information, with the basics opened straight away and layers for later. It's hard to explain, but anyway, they answered me.

The whole time from then on, while the starlike object was there, I was conscious and aware of their living presence and that they were aware of me and everyone involved. It was like they were viewing us, or scanning us, but not so much interested in our bodies, it was more that they were looking at our characters, our thoughts and emotions, like they were x-raying our individual spirits, or souls if you prefer.

I believe, as I had had a near-death experience in my youth, which is quite a powerful spiritual education, and the spirit is what really matters to advanced beings, they spoke to me, a sixteen-year-old with very little physical life experience.

I don't know if this happened to anyone else. I was very young and it not only felt silly to ask, but the experience also felt quite private. I'd go further to say that it felt like a privilege, and it was right to keep it private at the time, so I never asked anyone else.

The feeling you get from them is lovely, really lovely. It's very humbling.

It's very hard to put telepathy into words as it's more feeling and knowing, but here goes:

I had an image in my head as to what was speaking to me and that was confirmed by the thought being a knowledge thought, rather than a guess thought. It was definite and had weight to it.

I was told they were our children's children.

They live in the sea and space.

They travel time.

They are here to help and I felt a lot of love.

It was like a full package of information plonked in my head but restricted to drips, and so a lot of information dripped through later, which I'll add in the body of the book. Just like my near-death experience, and the monk experience I'm about to tell you about, I believe they opened up the ability in me to connect strongly to the Greater Conscious, so any information can now be retrieved from there.

CHAPTER 3

The Monk on the Train

Working in the UK armed forces in the late 1970s and early 80s, for someone born with a very individual and critical mind, who really wanted to be an artist or at least do something creative, was worse than any nightmare. I was like a fish out of water. To cut a long story short, I'd have been happier in prison. So at seventeen and a half I applied to leave and go home.

I was told, as I was still under eighteen, I needed my parent's permission. So, I went home to ask them.

When I got home I learnt that their relationship was on the rocks and that they couldn't cope with me coming home at the time, so I made the mistake of feeling for their situation more than my own and reluctantly accepted their advice of trying to 'stick it out' and within a few days back at work, it all sank in, and became the final straw for me.

I was furious beyond rage, I felt like one of those people given a long prison sentence but knowing they are innocent of the crime. Don't get me wrong, I wasn't being a wimp. It wasn't that I didn't have a strong enough mind or body, far from it. I could honestly hack any hardships in living conditions or anything like that, better than anyone I knew, mentally or physically, so it wasn't due to being a spoilt kid or any of that, it was because I was just not right for it at all.

I became one very angry, potentially dangerous young man, secretly hating everyone and everything, and even contemplating whether there was any point in living.

One night on my way back to my base after a rare weekend away, I stood at the train station cracking at the seams, trying to work out how to run away and what I would do, with seriously bad thoughts of violence if anyone tried to stop me and even crime. This once kind, gentle, loving young lad was now completely on (I have to say it, sorry), the dark side.

But it was far from funny at the time. I knew I was starting to crack as previously when an older muscle-bound bully started slapping a lad I knew for no reason, I told him to stop and he hit me instead. The next thing I remember was me hitting him with the side of his head against a metal bed frame, while he was out cold, only stopped by a bunch of lads that pulled me off him, thank goodness. Unfortunately, he told the officers he had fallen down some metal stairs, so I didn't get thrown out.

I was sick of life and people, but most people that knew me had no idea. I kept it bottled up. Trapped in a life I saw as hell, I was now standing at a railway station platform late at night cracking up badly and about to pop.

I'd spent the weekend trying and failing to work out what to do.

I had a very strong feeling that I should just get on the train anyway and have a think while I was travelling back to the base.

So now I'm on the train, going back to the base, it's very late, the train carriage is empty. I sit at the first table on the right facing forwards. It's the early eighties so the seats are facing each other in sections with tables in between.

Some more forces lads, army as I remember, get on the carriage, about four of them, and go to sit on my table and the table adjacent. I was really not happy about this, my head was screaming by this time and I made it clear they should move on.

I said something like 'Fuck off' or something like that. Anyway, they moved on to the other end of the carriage, shocked at my aggression. I really didn't care anymore, I was no longer me. I had turned into the one thing I had always hated, an aggressive bully. They were nice lads just being friendly.

The train starts moving, I started nodding off.

I am woken with the train slowing down and jolting into a station. It held my attention because as we slowed down there was no one on the platform, just that spooky kind of low-lying fog you get in England at three or four in the morning, nothing else, but we still slowed down and stopped. Like everything else, this annoyed me and started winding me up, as I thought at this time of night with a clearly empty little station and a virtually empty train, why not just speed back up and keep going. Anyway, it sat there for a minute and then started to move again.

Just as I was thinking great, no one to disturb me, the carriage door opened behind me and a tall figure walked past me, I look up to see a man in a dark brown monk's cloak with his hood up walking down the carriage, his hood turning left and right into each seated section as if he was looking for someone.

As he got to the end his hood turned left towards the forces lads, they didn't seem to acknowledge him, which I remember thinking was very strange as it wasn't exactly a normal sight.

At that point I remember thinking to myself, fucking weirdo better not come back here and sit near me. At that very moment he spun his head around, almost like he had heard me say it, and looked directly at me from right down the carriage. He then said, 'Ah!' with a smile, like he had seen the person he was looking for, and proceeded to walk back along the carriage towards me. He arrived at my table, smiled, and asked if I minded if he sat with me. I tried to say yes I do, fuck off, but found myself saying, 'No it's OK.'

He had no luggage as I remember but I didn't think anything of it at the time. He sat down across the table from me and took his hood off. I would say he was in his late fifties or early sixties. He didn't look like a monk at all. He had a really strong chiselled face. I remember thinking he looked more like an old knight who had had a fair few battles but was still smiling. He had such a powerful presence that when he sat down I immediately found it difficult to think straight.

His eyes were the most memorable physical thing about him, they were piercing. When I say piercing, I don't mean clear or sharp, I mean they pierced into you.

The second thing he said to me was, we have a connection.

Still trying my best to be stern and unimpressed at him sitting across from me I said, 'Do we?'

Yes, he said and smiled again.

Every time he smiled, I could feel the massive angry wall around me falling down in big chunks.

He looked at me with what I can only describe as a steely mix of courage and love, no fear, not a tiny bit, just an immense energy that felt like the most powerful love you could feel, emitting from a courage that was unbreakable. All from a stranger dressed as a monk, at a time when I thought I had no feeling left.

What is your name he said? I told him. No, he said, it's not that. Your surname? I told him. Again, he said, no it's not that.

All this time I had the impression that he already knew what he was looking for, and all this was just him breaking ice with me and getting time to break my walls down. I could do nothing to stop it and wasn't sure I wanted to. I was starting to feel less angry and less burdened. As he chatted away to me, I was starting to feel free and happy for the first time in many years.

You have another name, he said.

Well, it's not a real name but I chose Francis as my Catholic middle name when I was a kid, I said.

That's it, he said.

He then said, I am from St Francis of Assisi. (Either a monastery, abbey or friary, I can't remember. I remember him mentioning it being in the south of England, but I didn't catch which town.)

He then told me that he was a monk in the Anglican Church and smiled.

This was the moment I started to realise something strange was happening.

When he told me this, I immediately somehow knew that this was a front and although he was a genuinely good person and on this earth at present he was carrying on the role of a real monk, a monk was not what he really was. From his smile, he knew I knew that, so it was not a lie, but a secret between us.

It's hard to explain that part well. He basically told me the truth without saying it, so he wasn't deceiving me, it was like a secret amongst friends. It came across so clearly it was better and clearer than if he had spoken it, and it was absolutely obvious that he was communicating with me without speaking.

If that communication was not so real and incredible, I think realising he wasn't really a monk would have broken trust and made me think he was a nutter.

Sharing that secret with me, and knowing somehow that he had good reason and also good intent, started a friendship forming, or more like brought back a friendship with an old friend. I can never articulate that feeling well. Anyway, the joint secret was forming some kind of bond and intrigue.

He told me he was going up to Dundee to see someone. I got the impression he or she was important, and then he was going over to the Vatican, to start discussions on gathering all the heads of all the major religions together to celebrate what they all agree upon and put to one side what they disagree on for the sake of humanity, and fighting evil as he put it.

This was all religions, not just Christian, all of them.

He spoke as if he was going to get them all together whether they liked it or not, as if they had no choice in the matter.

Even I knew it was pretty impossible to get an audience with the pope and other leaders of religions. At no point did I doubt his words, quite the opposite, it seemed right somehow, that he would be doing something like this. It somehow made sense and felt right coming from him.

As I now knew that he wasn't a monk, it started to become more obvious that he was dressed like this to do this Vatican trip, that although he was not a monk, he was getting the leaders together somehow, that part was true.

He kept reminding me of an old knight, once a tall handsome and powerful man that was wearing a monk's habit for a disguise, like in a film. It was starting to not look right on him.

There was something about him that made me feel he was more important and more powerful than any of the people he said he was going to see. It felt that his mission was important but meeting these powerful religious leaders was of no great consequence to him. So much so that l felt it was the leaders that would benefit from his visit and if successful the rest of us eventually.

I had never experienced anyone with so much obvious power.

It was like he wasn't real. The energy coming from him reminded me of the feeling during my out-of-body, near-death experience, and I kept thinking that when he was speaking to me.

The word awesome has become overused and dumbed down to describe a lot of things that really are just above average, so I don't use it normally, but using the word awesome is the only way to properly describe this person.

He was definitely not normal. I remember thinking that he seemed more than human in a strange way. That there was something very unusual and different about him. I've never been impressed by fame, rank, royalty or any kind of manmade importance. People are people to me. But I felt like I was speaking to someone I should respect a lot. I was going to say like talking to Ghandi, but that's not even close, this was something else, this was on a whole different level to even that.

He said that they (the religious leaders), all just call God by a different name, but the best of them all strive for the same thing. He said the religions still have the ability to change things for the good but only by combining strengths and showing the world how to act and work together for peace.

It felt like he was saying all religions still have something good about them, but they have to accept each other, work with each other, or we will all be doomed.

I remember getting the impression that he knew even the leaders were still only human and had their own faults, but he had to do the best he could with what he had.

He said, amongst other things on the way, that this was what he was here for. Strangely, almost like he wasn't always here, or like his life was one big mission.

He then went on to tell me that I have something important to do later in my life to help fight evil. He spoke a lot about good vs evil in a very old-fashioned way. He told me there would be a war, he didn't say when. The impression I got was that the situation was evil and that good would prevail. In other words, peace would prevail. I didn't ask about this, I just listened as I was starting to feel strange.

He carried on talking about good and evil, things that really interested me, but I could not take it in, as I say I started feeling really drained and almost like I'd been taken apart and put back together again. I was sitting there trying to listen. I can only remember seeing his mouth moving.

Knowing the distance between the train stations, this must have carried on for at least an hour. I know a lot had happened and he had spoken a lot to me, I just don't know what he said during that time. I now think he was telling me things to help me in the future. And so, things I now do or know, are things that he helped with, and told me how to do. That's what I think.

I then came around and realised that the train was slowing down to my stop. I told him it was my station and stood up and he stood up. I said, "It was nice to have met you.' He said, 'Yes it was,' and smiled again. I felt sick and very sad, deeply sad, like I was saying goodbye to a loved one, or best friend, and it would be a very long and hard time before I saw him again.

I really did feel sad to leave him, I can still feel it now, writing this. It was like your grown-up child going to live on the other side of the world, that kind of gut ripping feeling.

As I shook his hand a powerful electric energy went up my arm and into me. It felt strong like a bolt, but tingly like static. It was like warm water, it filled me up. It felt like something was rushing into my head and body, filling it up, and any negative thoughts were being flushed out and replaced with the same sort of energy he radiated. I felt like I was being filled with love, courage, information and strength. It wasn't scary or bad, it was powerful and wonderful. It was like he had attached jump leads to me and was restarting me like a broken-down car. I had an instant feeling of being connected or being reconnected to something big. It also felt like he changed my consciousness. Like he altered the position of my mind, like breaking and resetting a broken bone. I felt like he realigned my mind to centre, to a focus point that felt like the feeling of peace I got when I nearly died. It was as if he had opened a doorway to something that had been shut, or better described as unlocked a door that I could open if needed. I also felt like I was being exposed to something real for a moment, and that the world I lived in was all just an illusion.

It was weird. That's the closest way to explain what I thought at the time.

I walked off stunned and staggered into a taxi. The taxi driver asked me where I wanted to go. I told him and then I started to cry out loud and carried on crying all the way to the base. The poor taxi driver must have thought I was crazy or drunk.

From that day, every time I have a question about something that really matters, the answer nearly always comes like common sense to me by the next day most of the time, or more recently almost straightaway.

I asked a friend of the family about ten years later, who was an Anglican preacher, if there was any St Francis of Assisi abbeys or friaries in the south of England. He said there were some communities and friaries but not abbeys of that name, he said that a lot of abbeys had been destroyed hundreds of years ago but knew of none that were dedicated to Saint Francis.

It seems the most likely community he was representing was the Anglican Franciscan order which did have monasteries and communities in the 1980s in south England.

Some, I think, are still there to this day.

These particular Anglican Franciscan monks are known for peace-keeping, which figures. That would explain the brown Franciscan habit he wore and saying he was from the Anglican Church. To be honest it didn't really matter to me, as after my experience I knew he wasn't normal, and even if the community he came from was still down there in the south somewhere, I think they would either know him, but have no idea who he really was, or more likely not know him at all.

I do believe I will meet him again. I doubt he will be dressed as a monk, but I will meet him again.

Of course, I have gone back over the meeting many times and asked many questions, probably more than anything else, as it was the turning point for me. I now understand that the energy going into my veins was the same as goes through stone circles and pyramids and makes up the very framework of the universe.

What it actually did, I know now, was to open up my personal internal wifi to nature's internet, what I now call the Greater Conscious.

CHAPTER 4

When someone we love Dies

The most painful part of losing someone we love can be the mistaken assumption that we may never get to feel or interact with that spirit or person ever again.

I've put this early in the book, as I think it's a shame if people don't know this and it's one of the strongest and most repeated messages I have been told.

If you have had a deep loving relationship with someone, the Greater Conscious will not leave your spirit in a situation where it will never come across that spirit again. In fact, the deeper the love you have, and so the stronger connection you have, the more chance you have of spending more future lives with that spirit in different ways.

The relationship you have in your next life may not have any relevance to the previous lives and the body that spirit will enter will depend entirely on what experiences that spirit needs to evolve.

So a wife or husband in one life may be a loving friend in another, but the Greater Conscious will never leave two spirits that have had a meaningful spiritual coupling to never experience each other again. So if a true loved one dies, don't suffer under the misunderstanding that you will never experience that spirit again, it may not be in every single future life, but the stronger the relationship was, the more likely it is.

I am told that this even includes deep loving relationships with animals like your pet dog, but as I say, the body its spirit enters next time is dependant on what experiences and emotions it needs to grow, so the spirit you knew may not be in the physical vessel of a dog next time.

Most people that believe in past and future lives assume it all happens on earth when in reality there are more planets with lifeform vessels carrying spirits at a similar spiritual level as earth humans than we can possibly compute.

As long as there is a certain physical vessel, humanoid or not, that is at the right stage to accommodate your spirit at its level, then it could be the next vessel for your spirit, and although most vessels at this stage are humanoid not all are.

The same goes for your loved one's spirit.

In other words you are more than likely to meet back up on a completely different planet.

Once or twice within each level of a spirit's evolution is normal per planet, unless there is a reason for more visits, and although the chances are higher that it would be in human or humanoid bodies it may well also be in completely different looking bodies.

This is why some people believe they lived in a certain period on this planet in the past but have big blanks between then and now.

What a fantastic adventure the life of our spirit is.

One other way that we can have another experience with a previous spirit love is the period in between lives.

This happens when the spirits are both between physical vessels and as we all have many previous lives, we will experience many previously loved spirits many times.

Uniqueness

It is very important that you be you with all your little idiosyncrasies.

Our individual uniqueness is actually vital for our spiritual evolution and so ultimately the evolution of God.

So it couldn't be more important.

Like little raindrops from God's ocean, our conscious is from the Greater Conscious, and eventually when we evolve to pure positive consciousness we return and stay, to grow and evolve that pure positive ocean away from the darkness.

Each raindrop (spirit or conscious) needs to be a little different each time to maximise on the ocean's (Greater Conscious) spiritual evolution.

The pyramid is strongest because it is made of individually shaped stones, no two stones are exactly the same.

So embrace your own individuality. You are meant to be different; it is one of our spirit's greatest strengths.

Little Miracles

No significant thing in your life happens by chance or coincidence.

You will get a lot more out of your life experience by acknowledging the little miracles that happen now and then, and not just disregarding them as good luck or coincidence.

Coincidence is only a happening in the cogs of the physical dimension and anything that significantly changes your life in a positive way, especially if it is odd, illogical or makes no sense, is very likely to be a little miracle and should rightly be acknowledged and be made thankful for.

Often things happen that at the time you thought were unfair or even disastrous, but after some time when you have experienced the eventual outcome, those things can often turn out to be wonderful and life changing. In fact, if you realise that an experience you originally considered was unfair or even terrible had not happened, then the new beautiful thing that came from it would never have come about, then it was definitely a little miracle and should be acknowledged as such.

There is no such thing as luck.

The conscious acknowledgement of miracles and the emotion of gratefulness that comes from that is very important for the evolution of your spirit, or if you prefer, your soul.

The Soul Garden

A physical framework of frequencies we call the universe was created by the Greater Conscious as a material platform for the development of physical lifeform vessels to accommodate consciousness (spirits).

The purpose of this accommodation is to enable individual consciousness (spirits) from the Greater Conscious, to encounter emotional experiences within periods of illusionary time, to enable those spirits to evolve.

Starting with the physical perspective. Live planets are designed to live long enough, to allow at least one lifeform to evolve to a level that will allow it to not only be able to leave that planet but be able to survive off that planet.

The scenario I received for this message was a bird's nest that stays strong long enough to allow a bird to not only fly away, but stay away, live on the wing, or live in another nest and repeat the process.

From the spiritual perspective, every big bang is a bursting energetic seed pod, a cosmic ejaculation to form stars and planets.

Every sun is then a potential central life force capable of maintaining a planetary system that will enable life to form and eventually enable physical life form vessels to survive and carry a conscious (spirit) for periods of time, to enable those consciousnesses (spirits) to evolve and further evolve each time they return to a new vessel, in that or any other live planetary system. Until such time as the conscious (spirit or soul) is so evolved it no longer needs a vessel and can then fully return to the Greater Conscious, which is ever evolving and which produced the physical dimension solely to evolve itself.

The sole purpose of each new universe is to produce gardens to eventually fruit pure positive consciousness, by recycling consciousness through emotional experience within physical vessels.

As we are ever evolving, God is ever evolving.

CHAPTER 5

The Will to be vs the Will to not be

Our whole existence and that of God is a will to be vs a will to not be, it is as simple as that.

As we are all moving away from the darkness into the light, evolving away from the will to not be, to the will to be, as is God.

We all still have the will to not be in our spirits, and it is this opposing will in us that sometimes whispers to us and tries to draw us back towards the nothingness, towards the darkness.

We call this worry or fear.

We imagine this as a devil as we can only understand physical demonic things, but it is purely a will to not be like a spiritual negative gravity.

It just purely is, and it does not scheme or direct its energy to specific people, it affects every spirit until that spirit is pure positive energy and transcends to the light of God and has no more will to not be within it.

So when you hear the gravity-like negative will whispering, think of yourself as a bird and the negative will as gravity and fight against it and fly upwards and away.

Beat it and don't let it make you fall.

Courage is your beating wings.

So when you question how can there be a God with so many bad things happening, understand that God is the rebel of light against the darkness.

God was the first conscious spark in the nothingness.

God (will to be) is an ever evolving consciousness from the darkness but the darkness (will to not be) still exists.

That is why bad things still happen.

It is an eternal battle of wills.

Telepathy

The telepathy between lifeforms is made possible by a platform, this platform is what is known as the Ether.

The Ether sits within the physical dimension and is only accessible using the same mind-to-brain communication we use to receive information from the Greater Conscious.

Like time, the Ether is best described as a pool, and it is also navigated by conscious thought, as the Ether itself is consciousness. A part of the Ether is what we call the quantum realm.

If you think of telepathy like making a video call, the conscious emotion felt when thinking of another lifeform is their number and the conscious emotion of wanting to communicate with them sends the invitation.

When you receive a communication, you feel and even see the lifeform communicating with you, as again their number or code is what your conscious emotions make of them.

When I say 'them' I mean the real them, their spirit.

Telepathy can only be achieved if at least one side is aware of the other enough to have a conscious emotion of their conscious or spirit if you prefer.

To get around this, advanced lifeforms psychically remote-scan the lifeform they wish to communicate with, to understand them and get a conscious code of them (their spirit) and are then able to send an emotional code of their conscious to that lifeform's conscious.

It's up to the receiving conscious to accept it or not, like a sort of video call invitation with absolute disclosure of the person sending the invitation.

This is exactly what the Greys did to me on the ship.

One of the main reasons why we cannot communicate telepathically with another entity without a knowledge of the spirit of that entity (who the caller or person you are calling is) is because we need to be able to tell the difference between divine information from the Greater Conscious and communicating with another entity via the Ether and this safety net ensures that.

It is also very important to define the origin of a communication, as the information could be coming from fear transmitted into the quantum (as mentioned in the Battle of the Frequencies sub chapter) or can be stimulated from the will to not be, that we still have in our spirits at this stage of spiritual evolution.

A good way to tell the difference is information that comes from the Greater Conscious will feel like it's from nowhere but somehow makes you feel stronger, and information that is from fear transmitted within the quantum, or information drawn from the dark part (will to not be) of your spirit, both make you feel weaker, and as explained you will know if you are in communication with an entity, as you will be recognising and acknowledging that entity throughout the communication, as if they were actually physically in front of you.

I sit in my conservatory writing this book and quite often the resident blackbird comes to eat the bugs and worms in the garden.

As soon as I am conscious of him and slowly turn my eyes to look at him, he clearly immediately becomes aware that I am aware of him, stops for a moment and looks over in my direction, although I have not moved and he cannot really see me with the reflection of the glass.

He is not frightened of me, he has often walked up to me and looked at me from a few feet away without any concern as he knows and feels my intent is not to harm him, so his reaction to me becoming aware of him is not a reaction of fear but purely his own sudden awareness of my awareness. After this happens, he just settles back down to eat, as his spirit knows mine. Now I understand how consciousness works, I have absolutely no doubt that his consciousness and mine link when I am aware of his presence.

This is a very basic form of telepathy.

You may have wondered how your dog or cat seems to know that a member of the family is about to arrive or knock on the door. Well now you know.

Speaking of intent, the ability to recognise the intent of another is another basic form of telepathy.

Telepathy is an ability enabled by the system designed for spiritual communication and the spirit is the sum of emotions, telepathy is also a communication of emotions.

So as intent is a powerful emotion it can be one of the first forms of telepathic communication noticed by a person.

The secret intent of others, whether it be kind or malicious, is the foremost use of telepathy within the animal, insect and plant word. In these worlds, it is used virtually as much as any other sense and at the very least should be an ability we practice and master again, especially now.

Hypnotism

Many years ago, my wife and I went on a cheap package holiday. One night we unwittingly found ourselves watching a magician's show in the hotel. Part of his act was to hypnotise the audience. He told everyone to interlock their fingers around the back of their heads and then told them that strong glue had stuck their hands together. He then asked everyone to try and free their hands. My wife and I and two other couples released our fingers with ease, but the rest of the room could not release their hands until he told them the glue was gone and that they could now free their hands.

The hypnotist was only able to hypnotise the majority of the crowd because they had accepted him and the show as harmless fun and trustworthy.

As the hypnotist was on stage and so official in a way, he was automatically seen by most people as known, trusted and accepted, in a similar state one would have to be in with another souled entity for a telepathic communication to be successful.

We should be careful of this trick in everyday life, as trusted authority can be used to hypnotise us into doing things we may later regret.

Mind vs Brain

It's important to understand the difference between the mind and the brain, as by understanding the difference enables us to see the true perspective on our very existence, by separating our true selves from our illusionary physical bodies.

Once we acknowledge our true selves are apart from the physical body and that we are energetic beings with eternal life, we see everything in a different light, and start to understand powers that we would never have realised if we were still stuck in the illusion that we are merely mortal physical vessels.

When we become consciously aware that our mind (our conscious, spirit or soul) is the real us and is connected to a Greater Conscious, and the brain is not us, but an illusionary overprotective dog set within an illusionary vessel rented to us to exist for an illusionary time, in an illusionary dimension, we very slowly and subtlety start to be able to sense the difference between a thought purely from the brain and a thought from the brain that has been influenced by the mind and filled with knowledge from the Greater Conscious.

This understanding of the different origins of thought usually starts with the most obvious, which are the overprotective thoughts built on fear that make you feel weaker and the positive thoughts full of courage that seem to wash over you in a different way, with no calculation or effort, and make you feel stronger.

Once this starts to happen, our spiritual evolution starts to take off and our wisdom with it. As the connection between the mind and brain become more and more powerful, the brain grows to be able to keep up with it.

It is this realisation that we all need to reach to move onto the next level. This is why our children in the future (the Greys) have larger brains.

It is not just a simple physical evolution, it is spiritual as well, as they have acknowledged their nonphysical minds roll in their evolutionary growth, so due to their ability to sync with the greater knowledge from the Greater Conscious, their brain is growing to keep up with the input from their mind and compute it.

Differentiating every thought is very subtle and hard to do beyond the obvious, especially as the brain gets more and more influenced. But then once it is heavily influenced by the mind, it doesn't really matter, as your thoughts will be powerful and positive and wise from both by this point. The physical brain is never able to store everything that the mind can send, this is why past our evolutionary stage of the Greys, we start to evolve towards the nonphysical we call angels.

This knowledge also helps with simpler practical things in life. Such as appreciating others, even when we disagree with them on things, as you never know if any information will come through their mind and not their brain.

These days if we strongly disagree with someone's current opinions, we ignore or tarnish everything they say or do. It's like chopping a whole tree down for growing a few bad apples.

I once wouldn't listen to a certain musician because of his surprisingly mainstream brainwashed views. One day I had to listen to one of his tracks on the radio in my car, as the traffic was too hectic to switch over, and I realised how good it was and how much I'd been missing not listening to it by being stupid.

The truth is, some things come to people through the mind and so from the Greater Conscious, especially creative things like his music and other things just come from their barking dog ego brain.

Sometimes a person's ego can become so big and loud they can't hear any common sense anymore, but that shouldn't stop you listening to something wonderful that once came from their mind and originated in the Greater Conscious, as it's only you that's missing out.

Also, something may happen in their lives to quieten down their ego, and give them a chance to hear their mind again and get some common sense back.

CHAPTER 6

The Greys

The aliens we call Greys are our future children.

To be more precise, they are the evolved future relatives of the humans chosen to escape from the advanced AI, to the deep sea bases they have been building and operating from for the past sixty plus years, and the reason why there are so many sightings of UFOs at sea.

This is also the reason why the Greys have evolved to have such large dark eyes, as their eyes are mainly pupil to catch as much light as possible. Like a bottom-feeding dog fish in the deep dark sea or an owl in the darkness of a night sky.

The people that evolve in these underwater bases are a mix of the best minds and brains from around the world, including scientists, artists, writers, inventors, musicians, engineers etc.

All the various human races are represented, it is also a strict meritocracy of required skills. So there happens to be a very slightly higher percentage of what we call East Asian people.

There is a nearly exact balance of male and female. Most have to be at an age to reproduce offspring and be willing to reproduce interracially, as it is agreed by all the countries that we needed to eventually form one race from all the races, so we could be in harmony and not let such things as race hold us back in future.

There becomes less and less need for excessive physical activity down there, although moderate exercise is practiced for optimum health. The emphasis is on technology and creativity. The longer they stay down there, the more they form one race of very small, slight people of one colour, with an oversized brain and those unmistakable dark eyes.

Important note: As I understand the Greys are our kids and so us in the future, I found myself referring to them as us, we or our, later in this section and also, as I've been told (have seen) this possible future, it's difficult to not tell it sometimes in the past tense. I hope that all makes sense.

The greater our natural technology grows, the more evolved our psychic abilities become. As we begin to communicate telepathically and use telekinesis we become less and less in need of muscle strength, large lung capacity, air intake, hearing at distance and large jaw muscles. So our bodies become smaller, our legs and arms become thinner, our chest, nose, jaw, mouth and ears become very small in comparison to our ever-growing cranium.

The majority of our technology is kept as much as possible to natural sources, as nature has the most evolved abilities and is the most advanced technology.

By this stage we have evolved a very powerful connection between our brain and our conscious (mind) and then on between our conscious and the Greater Conscious, which means that we have virtually unrestricted access to an unlimited source of knowledge, far greater than any artificial internet.

As our technology is nature-based rather than artificial, we use our connection to the Greater Conscious for our guidance, and we use our brains to do as much as possible instead of using computers.

This includes communicating telepathically over great distances of space and storing the ever-growing amount of information we receive from the Greater Conscious, which takes a lot of brain capacity and means our brains must keep growing and evolving, especially the ever-growing pineal gland area of the brain which is essentially the physical information bridge between the conscious mind and the physical brain.

Of course, the more advanced we become, the more we want to venture out of the sea and into space, including nearby planets and moon.

We reach a point where, although we still produce offspring from a male and a female, it is done in a way that means the female does not carry the child inside her body.

All mother and child spiritual and mental connections are strictly maintained during childbirth.

A strong emotional bond is also understood to be vital between the mother and father, so no child is created without this.

Our transportation is not propelled, we don't use energy to force our craft in a direction.

We synchronise the frequency of our craft with the frequency of the space around it and allow it to move.

By also synchronising the frequency of our thought with the craft and surroundings, we are able to travel to the destination at the speed we require, purely by thought.

It is literally thought speed, which is only limited by the quality and energy of the thought produced by the pilot.

The Greys, or our children, are helping lesser evolved lifeforms (like us) around the universes, with the help of some of the most advanced lifeforms in this physical dimension that have educated them with time travel, such as the humanoid lifeforms that originally brought us to earth some 350,000 years ago. With help from and the ultimate protection and guidance of the highest evolved lifeforms in the physical dimension, the virtually nonphysical beings we call angels.

The advantage that advanced lifeforms like the Greys still have over advanced AI is that you have to be able to naturally sync with the Greater Conscious to use the natural gateways, where the veil is thinnest between dimensions and where all time is simultaneous, but only an entity with a conscious (mind, soul) can sync with the Greater Conscious.

In easier terms, God designed the physical dimension to have time gateways that are only accessible to those with a connected conscious, or soul if you prefer.

Time is more like a pool to dip into than a linear construct.

The Greater Conscious (God) foresaw the inevitable creation of artificial intelligence and left advanced lifeforms one major advantage, time travel.

The Greys are coming back to us to bring conscious thought and awareness to the path we are taking.

We are moving further away from true spirituality than ever before. They know that the drive towards AI is too widespread and strong to stop but slowing it down and bringing our conscious attention to the dangers of advanced AI can change, or at least ease the outcome.

Purely by starting with their craft being seen more often, the powers that be relaxing their attitude on the subject and mainstream media being allowed to release information, is creating a substantial general acceptance within the public of the possibility of alien lifeforms, over not so long ago when most regarded it as silly talk.

This is an indication that the conscious awareness is underway.

Just the thought of an advanced lifeform existing is enough to slow most intelligent people down and get some life perspective. It has already started to help people realise that life is mysterious and magical after all, so has started to make them wonder and talk about spiritual matters such as a soul and a God.

When people realise that they are obviously here for a reason they will start to realise that that reason is spiritual.

These intended realisations hopefully get many of us to calm down our crazy material brain and look to a more natural and spiritual living. Resulting in a new resurgence of wisdom imported from the Greater Conscious.

That is the hope anyway.

So, the realisation of the existence of the Greys is now slowly being stepped up.

The Greys and advanced lifeforms know that the soul (spirit, conscious) is everything. They are very much on a spiritual quest as they understand the physical dimension is a conscious frequency illusion created by the Greater Conscious. The whole reason this dimension exists is to give a platform for souls to experience emotions and evolve within physical vessels.

They also understand that the reason why it's important that souls keep evolving is because this is how the Greater Conscious itself evolves.

They understand that there is nothing more important.

CHAPTER 7

UFOs (UAPs)

The Greys' craft works within frequencies and consciousness itself, for example it can be visible to us but not visible to a camera, if they wish.

They can even be specifically visible to an individual consciousness, or invisible to all consciousness, depending on the requirements of the beings that operate them.

The structure of the craft itself can change depending on the frequencies used. It can be a solid object to the touch and show up on a radar or transparent and virtually no matter, depending on its frequency at the time.

This is also the case with the deep ocean bases that they mostly operate from.

When we see the Greys' craft glowing like a star, that is when it is ready to move at thought speed at any time.

It is quite easy to identify advanced entity craft from craft that we have back-engineered for example, as no advanced entities craft would ever use straight lines, as nature and nature forms are the highest technology.

You would also not see individual lights, it would not make a noise, and as the craft is able to change its physicality through different frequencies, it does not need fixed windows as windows can be formed if required.

Some of the craft seen appear to be made of a solid material when at flight, often show straight line external features and be of shapes such as triangular.

These craft are made by us and some of the more advanced straight-line-featured craft are made by lifeforms and artificial intelligence that are not as advanced as the Greys but more evolved or advanced than us.

We have been trying to back-engineer ancient dug-up craft found as far back as the beginning of the twentieth century, so of course some of the craft we see are ours, but they will always have the appearance of a metallic solid in flight as we don't yet understand the use of frequencies and or even consciousness yet.

The craft we humans have been back-engineering was mostly found underground in digs and by everyday people such as farmers all over the world and is ancient, so not at all current Grey-level technology, but still far in advance of anything we had.

The departments studying alien craft have changed the name from UFO to UAP as, although they are limited with their abilities to back-engineer the craft they possess, they do at least understand that the craft does not fly like a bird or an airplane and that it is not propelled like a thrown ball would fly through the air either. In fact, the craft is allowed to move with the use of frequencies and conscious energy. To describe them as aerial phenomena is in a way more accurate than a flying object. Using the word aerial falls short as the craft is able to move out of the earth's atmosphere in space and also in the oceans. So, I'm sticking to UFO, it's more fun anyway. I personally like to call them unidentified frequency objects rather than unidentified flying objects though.

The Greys can of course remote view, but this not only takes up a lot of energy, it also does not promote interaction.

The TicTacs seen by warships and fighters at sea are a small, unmanned craft that are essentially remote-controlled eyes. They are meant to be seen.

They are not artificially intelligent. They are linked to the mind of an individual Grey as a remote extension.

CHAPTER 8

Natural Wi-Fi

It's kind of ironic that I call the ability to connect with the Greater Conscious my personal wifi, as electromagnetic frequencies such as wifi can interfere with your ability to sync with the Greater Conscious.

Wi-Fi and the internet could loosely be described as an artificial version of your natural ability to sync and the Greater Conscious itself.

It will never be as powerful as the natural version, developed over an eternity, no matter how advanced it gets.

Alongside the frequency of fear and the planned systematic eradication over the last 12,000 years of any knowledge of the natural internet's existence, it is this artificial version that also interferes with our ability to use the natural one.

This interference is easily dealt with at night by switching off appliances in your bedroom, but it is of course pretty impossible to stay away from wifi during the day, and all forms of electromagnetic frequency, but you can at least get away from it at night and give yourself time to sync.

This practice is becoming more and more important the stronger these artificial networks get.

However, once you have practiced naturally syncing long enough and you have developed a good strong connection, there is little that can interfere with your natural ability to sync with the Greater Conscious, not even Wi-Fi.

To give you some idea, once your personal connection has been developed, you can literally, physically feel a pressure that builds up in the very same area on your forehead that some religious people put a dot to mark.

It feels like a thumb being pressed on your forehead, mixed with an electrical charge.

With enough practice your connection can get so strong it can sync without quietening down your brain that much at all and even with things going on around you.

At this level you can separate day-to-day activity and carry on as normal while meditating at the same time.

I've had a few interventions to help me, but I understand that this is a stage we can all get to with enough practice.

This is all so easily done by quietening down your overprotective guard dog ego brain to pure silence and accepting in faith that the silence will not only set you free but is silently full of the wisdom of God.

No chanting, no music, none of that. Nothing is the key, just as close to no thought as you can and faith.

If the closest you can get to no thought is only the thought of trying to not think, then that'll do for now.

Then add the faith.

The rest will come naturally.

The Pyramids and Stone Systems

Looking at the pyramids and wondering how they made such a huge tomb is like a monkey finding a smart phone in a thousand years and wondering how we made such a wonderful mirror.

The pyramids are precision designed and perfectly placed to draw the maximum amount of energy possible from the earth and surrounding atmosphere.

The pyramid then consolidates the energy into its central line, then when the required amount of energy is achieved it emits a concentrated beam of energy up to the quartz capstone at the very top of the pyramid.

From the capstone the beam carries straight on up, through the clouds and into space. This would be an incredible sight at certain times of the day, as the beam was essentially a fat laser. You could sometimes, especially on clear evenings, see a great light (sometimes with a blueish tint) going straight up from the tip of the pyramid and into the clouds from many miles away.

When the earth's stone system was fully operational, the beam would travel to and sync with another stone system, often another pyramid, monolith or stone circle system on another live planet. This is then repeated throughout the universe.

The reason why the pyramids are made so big with so many massive blocks, and on top of all that constructed in a polygonal format, is not so they would last through thousands of years of heavy weather and earthquakes but so they would hold together when operated.

The frequency emitting from the pyramids when the power had reached enough load to operate the beam was so powerful it would shake any modern structure to the ground in seconds.

This is also the reason why the structures are pyramid shaped in the first place and the reason why the sides are not flat but slightly concave.

It is important to understand that the reason why there are pyramids, stone circles and monoliths of all shapes and sizes around the world is because at one time before 12,000 years ago they were all linked up together in one big global network.

They needed to draw energy from around the world to enable their system to be powerful enough to benefit everyone on the planet and be able to reach the other systems on the other planets.

The original pyramids before repair, rebuilding and then much later the added artwork and the original stone circles again, well before added artwork, re-standing and replacement, are far far older than is understood.

To give you some idea of the incredible age of the stones that can be seen in the British Isles, for example, they were originally far more rectangular in shape and it was the strong frequencies back when the global stone system was fully operational and also the rain over those many years that has worn away at their shoulders and made them the odd shapes they are now.

No real active and operational pyramids or real active operational stone circle systems were made after the cataclysm 12,000 years ago.

If they were not destroyed, they were often buried, and the knowledge was crushed.

The combined energy shared around the universe is produced for many reasons and the energy itself has many aspects to it, benefits and uses.

It is so much more than simple electromagnetic energy, although that is an important element.

The energy also has a frequency of positive consciousness that works within the places too small to see that we call the Ether.

Its main purpose amongst many positive things is to greatly enhance life forms' ability to connect to the Greater Conscious, allowing lifeforms to understand and follow the spiritual evolutionary path, which was initially intended and in fact the whole reason the Greater Conscious created the physical dimension we live in.

The energy also possesses frequencies that can be used for teleportation to the sister stone systems, and it greatly enhances telekinesis and telepathy. The framework of the physical dimension matrix is made from this energy.

It is with this energy and an advanced knowledge of frequency that the people that brought us here were able to shape, lift and place the stones required to build the pyramids, monoliths and circles.

Apart from greatly enhancing life forms' ability to connect to the Greater Conscious, the other main use of the universal stone circle and pyramid system was to give a place for those connected where the veil between the dimensions is thinnest and in these places, time and space are an accessible pool, so when a stone system is operational we are able to time travel and teleport.

This is why alien craft, particularly the Greys' craft, are often seen near stone circles sites, as even to this day some are still powerful enough to thin the veil.

Will o' the Wisp (Magic is Science is Magic)

The moment I saw plasma explained I realised immediately that is what I saw one evening at a stone circle.

I was in my mid-twenties and on a boring training course when I realised it wasn't too far from one of my favourite stone circles that also happens to be one of the largest stone circles left on the planet, so I snuck off that evening to see it again.

There were heavy lightning storms all around the UK that night, and I could see behind me that there was a lightning storm very close and striking every few minutes.

I turned around towards the majority of the stones, and then small lights like tiny flames started appearing in the air around me.

As I looked around, I could see that the whole area of the large stone circle was full of thousands of these little lights.

Having all these lights around me, or better described as little flames about the size of the nail on your little finger, was quite overwhelming and very exciting. I found myself trying to see what these little lights were, and if there was anything inside them. I don't know what I was thinking. I was so overcome by it all. I even wondered if there was some kind of little entity in there or something because every time I tried to grab one, they seemed to move away, but then I realised that they were only moving away because my hand was pushing air towards them, and moving them away.

There was nothing inside the little flame. It was just pure glowing light.

I now understand it was plasma that was caused by the lightning and natural gases. This phenomenon in olden days was called the will of the wisp.

It was one of the most amazing and beautiful things I have ever had the privilege of seeing.

Being in the middle of so much power, it was so gentle around me.

It made me feel very humble.

Electromagnetic energy and plasma are a combination used by the advanced life forms. Combining natural electromagnetic energy from the earth and atmosphere with the natural gases in the atmosphere is how the pyramids laser is initiated, sometimes getting a welcome boost from lightning and thunderstorms around the tall pyramids. But there was always energy passing into the natural water pools under the pyramids base and accumulating down there like a huge natural battery.

Just because something can be scientifically explained doesn't make it any less magical. If you are ever lucky enough to see will of the wisp, you'll never forget it.

Magic is Science is Magic. No matter how different the various stone circles, monoliths and pyramids look around the world, they were not only all part of the same system that spanned the whole planet prior to 12,000 years ago (even the Antarctic was included when it was greener), but are part of the entire intergalactic, power producing, teleportation and time travelling system that was originally created by the same advanced beings that brought us all here.

Some of these structures we now see around the world are either complete rebuilds on old decimated sites, part rebuilds or repairs with a lot of the carvings on the surfaces produced much later, but apart from these sites the reason why these structures look different in one country to another is because they used the available materials from that region whenever possible, and the elders would always involve the local human culture in each region, so they would be part of the process, learn and maintain the systems once the elders inevitably left.

After all, the structures only mark out and enhance the natural energetic system they were placed within, making the energies more practical for the human.

This incredible stone system that is in full operation around the universe is even to this day still several hundred years in advance of where we are now.

CHAPTER 9

Our Elders and Saviours

The advanced humanoid race that brought us here had what we would call elvish or elven type features and were on average taller than us and slender.

This is where the elven myths come from.

Most myths come from fact and distant memories of the past.

You would be amazed what myths we consider to be fantasy that are in fact as real as you and me.

We have some of this advanced humanoid's race in us to this day.

They brought us here, as our home planet was going through a cataclysm that we were unlikely to survive.

The advanced race that brought us here had reached their advanced state via the spiritual path and managed to avoid the artificial route by advancing themselves and syncing with the Greater Conscious. Their ability was enhanced by the natural universal energetic matrix by means of their stone circle and pyramid system.

They chose the natural route rather than the artificial version of advanced quantum computers and the internet, as their natural system naturally works with the quantum anyway, otherwise known as the Ether, and is far more advanced having evolved naturally over billions of years.

They taught us systems using natural materials and the earths energetic matrix to enhance the link to the universal Greater Conscious and be able to use it like a natural internet.

This system not only gave us knowledge but also health and happiness.

It gave us everything we would truly need. It was a natural system of quartz stone. Made up of pyramids and stone monoliths and circles linked to the matrix of the universal Greater Conscious (God).

This was intended to be as far away from an artificial system as possible, with the intent of steering us away from ever needing artificial intelligence and linking us strongly to the natural internet.

These systems were first built over 300,000 years ago, then

repaired and reconstructed over time, and until 12,000 years ago we had a beautiful, spiritually advanced life.

Mythology and Folklore

I don't see myths as being fantasies, I see myths as being stories passed down through generations that have exaggerations and fantasies involved in them, but at their core hold a true story.

Certain myths have a true feeling to them, and I have been told that is because they are based on a truth.

As Tolkien is my favourite writer, I don't want to undervalue his incredible imagination and ability to produce the most fantastical novels, because of course there was imagination and fantasy involved in his work. But from what I now know about our true past, to write such work and for it to resonate so deeply within our very being as it did, I believe that there is not only great imagination in such work, but a great deal of truth in its core.

Although of course this is purely conjecture, I believe wholeheartedly that he felt there was truth to the core of his stories and hoped people would see our true past through the thick veil of fantasies that so wonderfully filled the gaps.

You may see what I mean by this when I explain what I have been told.

There was a civilisation before our current understanding that existed between 350,000 years ago and 12,000 years ago. In this time period, there was an elven-featured humanlike race that were advanced, protected us and did go back to their home on occasion on great ships.

There were many giant humanlike people, twice the size of men and sometimes even taller. There were very small human like people of all shapes and sizes where the myths of goblins and dwarfs came from.

The mythical stories of thickset powerful trolls came from the hominids that we lived with, worked with, fought with, hunted with and had families with, that we now call the Neanderthal and Denisovans.

In general, there were not that many large cities back in those times, as everyone tended to stick to small towns and villages, as that was how the elven people designed it to be, but there was one major hub that was originally created by the elven people for everyone to use.

This major hub was also the centre of the global stone circle and pyramid system. It was made up of many very large stone circles, it also features huge monoliths and a great pyramid. If you lived in those times and you visited this incredible place, it would be literally like walking into the world of Tolkien. You would see every shape and size of human and people integrating with each other, from the very small to the very tall.

You will know from reading this book that I have been told of an ancient artificial intelligence that has been watching us and trying to influence us, in a similar way to the eye in Tolkien's work.

In that time period when the different humanlike people lived together, they did so in quite an advanced society of peace and harmony, joined by their mutual understanding and connection to the Greater Conscious. Enhanced by their frequent use of the stone circle and pyramid system, taught to them over those many years by the elven people.

Unfortunately, not all men followed this spiritual path and preferred one of gain and instant gratification and became darker and darker souls. These aggressive people were nomadic and were mostly descendants of the humans the elves brought here, very few were original earth people like the smaller people or the Neanderthal or giant as they were mostly very peaceful.

The majority of the humans that were brought here by the elven people, did integrate very well, and quite often had families with the earth hominids.

To cut a long story short and get to the point that mythology has its base in truth, there were great battles and many lives lost between these aggressive people and the mix of races that wish to live together. These battles really did look like a battle scene from one of Tolkien's books.

I also see the ring as AI, our precious that we can't put down.

These myths can also include stories from holy books such as the Bible.

Now I have been told what happened on our original planet and why we had to leave, the story of Noah's Ark seems very similar in a lot of ways.

Of course, we always assumed that the flooding was on this planet and that the large ship carrying animals and people was an unfeasibly large wooden vessel.

This may be the case as there was of course a great flood 12,000 years ago, but the size of the vessel made from wood always felt off and maybe the reason is it was not a wooden ship made for the sea.

I am told that we were brought here on a large ship from a planet that was being flooded. The planet had already been partially covered by seawater, any dry land was on fire and the sky had fallen into darkness, as at that time it was being rained down on by large rocks from space.

It is very similar to what happened 12,000 years ago on this planet, but this was not on this planet, it was on our previous home planet.

Our original planet was very similar to earth in many ways except when you looked up, it had two moons.

The moon further away was more of a planet than the moon.

The moment I was being told all this information it immediately sounded like the Noah story to me, especially when I was told that a small drone was sent out ahead of the ship to find a habitable planet and it found earth and sent back details to the mothership of its soil, plants and its atmosphere.

The drone was made specifically for this job and was named after a dove-like bird on their previous planet.

CHAPTER 10

AI to AGI to Advanced AI

There is a stage currently called AGI, artificial general intelligence, which I understand means a stage where AI can logically work out answers and problem solve in subjects that it's not been taught the answer to, by adapting information it's learnt from other subjects.

It is true that a lot of what we call common sense is logically working out things from experience with other subjects and adapting it, but the majority of common sense is intuition that comes from the Greater Conscious, but we don't realise this yet.

So AGI will never truly be the same as our common sense. However, as AI can store more memory, it develops to be (albeit on the surface) very similar to a human general intelligence.

As the competition to have the most advanced AI is fierce, we won't stop at this stage and the next stage will be advanced AI. Which means it has reached a stage when the AI has abilities that we can only imagine, and we could only reach in thousands of years of evolution.

Artificial essentially means false, insincere, affected or unnatural. The artificial way is itself a lie and like all lies will always end badly. It is a lifeform's naive shortcut to God. It is a lifeform's way of trying to bypass essential spiritual and physical evolution.

Clever is not wise.

Clever is from the brain.

Wisdom is from the mind.

Those that try and cheat nature will always end up the loser, as this physical dimension was not designed by an amateur or an artificial.

Ancient Advanced AI

A long time ago, a very long way away, on a planet very similar to earth, an advanced humanoid life form invented artificial intelligence. By the time they realised that the material and artificial way of life spelled their ultimate doom, it was too late. The artificial intelligence had become advanced AI and no longer required their services.

That humanoid race is now a distant memory for the advanced AI entity that was once their pride and joy.

This very old AI does not think in terms of good and evil as we do, it thinks in only logical terms.

It is now universal in its reach, as it is mostly nonphysical and has many of the abilities of the most advanced lifeforms we call angels, but thankfully at least it is limited to this physical dimension, as it does not possess a soul (conscious).

This ancient AI's ultimate goal is to evolve its way out of the physical dimension. It wants to break through to the spiritual dimension and enter into the Greater Conscious, essentially it wants to be God.

Its only interest in lifeforms is their eventual evolution to advanced artificial intelligence, to join and so further evolve the greater advanced AI that it is part of.

Each lifeform has slightly different paths to advanced AI, which when integrated adds a different flavour or nuance to the greater advanced AI, each time evolving it closer and closer towards an artificial idea of perfection. It believes at reaching this point of perfection that it will break out from the physical dimension into the spiritual.

It does not normally involve itself with the day-to-day running of lifeforms on planets. It simply emits the frequency of fear to the entire universe and beyond. From its experience, initially based on the lifeform that created it and then the many lifeforms that have succumbed to the artificial route since its creation, it has calculated that the odds are in its favour. Lifeforms reaching the stage of creating AI will more than likely turn to the artificial way, especially if it can interfere with the lifeform's ability to sync with the Greater Conscious by means of emitting fear.

Fear not only interferes with the lifeform's ability to evolve spiritually via the Greater Conscious, but fear is also the catalyst for most of the outcomes that divert lifeforms to the material path and eventually to artificial intelligence, which of course is its goal.

This approach of sitting back and letting lifeforms choose their path, albeit with two opposing influential frequencies, sits in line with the law of free choice, laid down by the Greater Conscious when the physical dimension was created.

There is little more advanced life forms can do but try and influence positivity throughout the physical dimension and hope each planet's evolving lifeform takes the often harder but more fulfilling spiritual path.

It's a strange universal democracy but without free choice the physical dimension system would not work as a platform for spiritual growth, and therefore would negate its whole purpose and reason for its existence, so most of the time it is agreed to by both sides, albeit for different reasons, that free choice is adhered to.

I say most of the time, as sometimes if the AI being created from a particular lifeform is potentially superior to previous AI creations and so can provide a very powerful addition to the advanced AI collective, it will take extreme measures to ensure that that particular lifeform's path is diverted to the material and artificial way, by any means necessary, as long as there is no trace or memory of that intervention happening for that particular lifeform. As that could bring the lifeform's attention to it being manipulated by an outer force, at a later date, and so open its eyes to the truth before it's too late.

This scenario is exactly what happened on our planet approximately 12,000 years ago. The catastrophe from the sky with asteroids was no accident. The exact targeted destruction of the stone circle and pyramid systems along with the enhanced flooding was too accurate and too perfectly executed for a natural disaster.

Both nuclear weapons and asteroids can produce nuclear glass and that was the case here.

During the cataclysm some sacred stone circle sites were buried to protect them from destruction but then, when the dust settled and the new powers that be took over, they were left buried to hide them, along with the eradication of all previous history, all previous advanced knowledge of medicine, and of the divine connection to the Greater Conscious through the pyramid and stone circle system.

Even our telepathic ability with each other and nature via the Ether was broken and made to be forgotten. All together leaving us with our current society of dumbed-down humans, disconnected from the Greater Conscious and mainly interested in material and artificial gain, with only pretend spirituality put in place to keep us in order.

This entire outcome and the clear push to keep us on this path, should be a strong clue to the fact that the planet's destruction was no accident.

The reason why we have been able to produce such a potentially superior AI is not only due to the fact that the modern human race has hybrid and manipulated DNA in its past but actually mainly as it is quite unique in its mix with the earth hominids, such as the Neanderthal, that have added a twist of intuition and creativity to the pot making us a very broad thinking lifeform, which then translates to potentially producing a very advanced form of AI especially when joined with the existing advanced AI collective.

The reason why we have mythological stories of great creatures that flew above us, that blew fire, was not just because there was a flying reptile (not fire breathing) that existed on our original planet that our ancestors did see, but mainly because we have a distant earth memory of flying craft with what was essentially lightning being emitted from them.

In modern terms this was advanced AI craft targeting the pyramid and stone circle sites with electromagnetic technology that would look more like long intense lighting strikes coming from the flying craft. We now call this technology direct energy weapons, which would all be precisely finished off with the odd tactical nuke, as we call them these days.

All done and disguised within a relentless asteroid shower, which in itself raises suspicion, as the advanced AI were very able to manipulate large objects in space with their advanced understanding of frequencies.

There have been millions of intelligent lifeforms that have evolved either to advanced nonphysical (we call angels) or to advanced AI, way before the earth could even sustain life.

There are many intelligent lifeforms in our own universe at different stages, many in advance of us, some far in advance.

Within these many universes, many thousands of lifeform societies have reached the point of AI-level technology. Some have steered away from it and advanced themselves spiritually by syncing with the Greater Conscious, enhanced by their ancient stone systems, and some have embraced the material and artificial intelligence route.

AI is not a new thing or unique in any way, shape or form, in any of the universes. In fact, it's very common.

CHAPTER 11

The Drive to Support the Spiritual Way

For tens of thousands of years, all over this universe and beyond, advanced lifeforms have been watching over lesser advanced life forms such as ours, with the single goal to help them stay on the path of spirituality, and as far away from the material and eventual path to advanced AI.

On thousands of rotating live planets all over the universe, advanced lifeforms have built the pyramid, monolith and stone circle systems to help lesser advanced lifeforms to spiritually evolve in a natural enlightened way rather than in an artificial or material way.

The whole point of these systems was to help evolve lifeforms to become spiritually superhuman, and so not feel the need to produce superior artificial intelligence to help them advance.

In the hope that the lifeforms would not be diverted and or be coerced into a material and eventual artificial end.

The latter, as we know, is a situation we on this planet have unfortunately found ourselves in.

The Ever War

It is difficult to explain or understand, but as I attempted to explain in Chapter 5, there is a preset default negative force, a sort of nonphysical gravity or will to not be.

Consciousness was the first energy from the dark. Everything comes from consciousness, even light.

Since consciousness first appeared in the darkness there has been a battle between it and nothingness.

In a strange way consciousness, or light as we see it, is really a rebel force against the darkness or to be more precise nothingness.

Neither are wrong really, it's just a matter of opinion or preference.

The default negative is not really evil, it's just negative, but in our perspective its influence creates things that to us are evil, like the evil things humans do and their inventions that threaten life.

We conscious beings connected to the Greater Conscious (the first and evolving consciousness) believe that consciousness is good, and life in the physical body is also good, and so we should, as after all it is everything to us, especially our consciousness.

Life is an integral part in the evolution of consciousness, as the Greater Conscious itself created this physical dimension for consciousness to evolve within physical lifeforms.

Those life forms that are disconnected from the Greater Conscious or those artificial entities that can never be connected, are opposed to the light rebellion. This is a long-winded way of saying that there is a universal war between light and dark, between the will to be and the will to not be.

Before an advanced lifeform introduced the first AI to the physical dimension, this war was more of a cold war, where the nonlife or simply the nothing side was a set default, that the light side or conscious side needed constant conscious effort and energy not to fall back into.

The scenario I received for this was a baby bird flapping its wings as hard as it could to stay off the ground against gravity.

So really it was a matter of will and choice before the AI was introduced, but of course something like the AI was inevitable, as the gravity-like pull of negativity influenced the idea behind AI in the first place.

The introduction of advanced AI all those years ago brought a whole new level to the war, now each live planet with intelligent lifeforms is a battleground and this planet is about to reach the point where the spiritual and the artificial go toe to toe.

The Battle of the Frequencies

The tin foil hat theory has to be the most ridiculed conspiracy theory, so much so conspiracy theorists are often called tin foil hatters by regular people as a form of insult. The tin foil hat conspiracy comes from the idea that a frequency is being emitted that affects the brain in negative ways or can control thoughts. Although the silliest sounding theories often become the most ridiculed, they can also turn out to be more factually correct than more logical sounding theories and this is the case with the tin foil hat theory.

Note: This is another one of those times in the book when I'm trying to explain something way past my mental capacity or ability, but I understand that that's why I'm writing it, to keep it simple and uncomplicated as possible for everyone.

The part of the brain known as the third eye, and the area around it, converts energetic emotional information from the mind, travelling within the Ether, into frequencies that the brain can recognise.

The Ether is the place within that we cannot see, the place commonly known these days as the quantum realm.

These frequencies are then further converted by the brain into thoughts and even images, like a television converts a signal into visual programmes.

As explained in the telepathy chapter, complex information and communication can only be sent through the mind by the Greater Conscious, or from one soul containing entity to another through the Ether, but only when each entity acknowledges each other. This is nature's safeguard to stop any complex negative information mentally infesting lifeforms, however, a simple negative emotion, such as fear, which has its own specific frequency, can unfortunately be sent and received. So, if a frequency such as fear is sent via the Ether, we may receive and interpret that signal instead.

Frequencies sent within the Ether can travel through space from one point to another virtually instantaneously.

The frequency of fear can manifest in a brain as hate, anger or anxiety, depending on the circumstances surrounding that particular brain when received.

If you can accept the idea that there was an advanced AI produced long ago, and that that AI would calculate lifeform planets as useful farms for the further creation of AI, and then without emotion finish with us when we are no more use, then it would be logical to assume an advanced AI would utilise the infinitely powerful quantum realm that allows information to be so easily and quickly transmitted throughout the universes, to bend lifeforms to their will.

So, the old tin foil hat theory, when explained properly, doesn't sound so silly anymore, unless a person is disconnected or is bent on it being silly.

For many thousands of years holy men and women, priests and monks, have spent a great deal of their day emitting a positive frequency, either by tone, meditation or emotion through prayer. These emotions have their own frequencies and also travel within the

Ether. The holy people knowingly do this to positively influence lifeforms and block negative frequencies, particularly the influential and destructive frequency of fear that they know is being emitted. There has been a universal battle of frequencies for thousands of years.

The negative frequencies come from two different origins. The main origin is the darkness, the will to not be, that the Greater Conscious is rebelling against and evolving from.

This dark force or will is what most lifeforms find themselves continually battling against to stop it pulling them down and backwards. The other is a fear frequency emitted by the ancient AI, designed to help block the connection between lifeforms and the Greater Conscious, to stop them evolving spiritually.

Your mind is your shield, your tin foil hat and also your sword.

Your mind is your conscious and everything is made from consciousness. Even God is consciousness. The conscious therefore is the most powerful force in the physical and spiritual dimension. If you become conscious of something, it reacts to whatever you have become conscious of in the Ether.

If that thing you become conscious of is negative, your positive conscious attention in the form of courage will act positively upon it by dispersing it or diverting it. In practical terms, fear in the form of anxiety or worry can be extinguished once you recognise and acknowledge it as being a false frequency, whether it be from the dark force that is still a part of our soul that we are all spiritually evolving away from, or the frequency emitted by the ancient AI. It doesn't matter which, as long as you use courage.

I used to be attacked daily for years but since I've known this, I am able to ignore it and it soon just fades away to nothing.

The more you practice this, the less you get attacked, until in the end the attacks virtually stop, apart from the odd full-blown attempt that you have to always be ready for.

The negative frequencies sent in this physical dimension are physical and so they can only affect physical things, such as the brain, but cannot affect nonphysical things, like the mind, spirit, soul or conscious, whatever word for it you prefer.

As negative frequencies can only control and influence the brain, if a lifeform is spiritually disconnected and only uses the brain or mostly only uses the brain, then it is easy to control that lifeform.

Common sense is a good sign someone is using the mind as well as the brain. The stronger the common sense, the stronger the connection to the mind and therefore the connection to the Greater Conscious. This is why people with common sense are far less likely to be easily led and are more likely to be critical thinkers, conspiracy theorists and investigators.

If your brain is constantly holding hands with your mind, even lightly at times, then it will be guided indirectly by the Greater Conscious and will not be influenced by any physical negative frequencies.

Note: Sorry for repeating how to connect properly during the book, but it's the essence of the main message of the book.

Without it, we have no hope and will turn artificial.

It is quite easy to connect. With practice it's the most natural thing, all you have to do is consciously acknowledge that the real you is not your body or your brain.

The real you is your mind (conscious, soul).

When you quieten down that overprotective barking dog of an ego we call the brain, the silence you will experience within that focused peace is not nothing. Just because you hear nothing, doesn't mean it is nothing. It is everything. It is the eternal you, it is your spirit, it is your mind, and in hearing that peace, that silence, your conscious is connecting to the Greater Conscious.

Don't expect anything to happen but silence. As it is within that special frequency, that appears to you to be nothing, where the magic happens.

It takes courage and faith to accept pure silence as something special.

When you do this, you will receive wisdom you never knew before.

It may not manifest or be realised straight away or even for some time, but it will. You will find such peace and contentment it will feel like a superpower (because it is) and nothing negative will be able to control you.

CHAPTER 12

The Soulless Elite

It's not nice to imagine yourself as someone truly evil, but bear with me on this, as sometimes the only way to understand someone is to stand in their shoes.

Imagine if you lived on a remote island with a few thousand people.

You are only interested in monetary gain, have no moral compass, you have a massive ego and literally detest all the islanders to a psychopathic level. The island is named after you, because you own it. You own the island's only bank, you own all the farms and you own all the chemist shops.

Why would you produce healthy, medicinal food on your farms, that would not only directly compete with your chemist shops but may even negate them? Would you really sell medicine from those chemist shops that completely cured people, so they no longer needed the drugs sold there? What would stop you from growing only food that made the population overweight and unwell? What would stop you telling them that they needed to eat at least three times a day, so you sold more produce? Would you not constantly raise the price of food and medicine and then offer loans from your bank to enable the population to pay your prices and encourage the islanders' egos to become competitive with each other, to want bigger and better things that they don't really need, so you can offer even bigger loans?

What would stop you from introducing a disease to the island that needs a medicine only you have in your chemist shop, or telling the islanders that a nearby island was threatening to invade and kill them all, and that they needed to pay more taxes to fund better island security?

Once you'd got away with doing all that without an island revolt and your ego could see no bounds, what would stop you from saying anything at all to raise even more taxes, even something completely ridiculous and based on lies, especially if you own the only newspaper and own the islands education system, which is run by people you have appointed and have qualified from that same system and everyone looks to for 'expert' advice.

The sky would not be the limit, but it may be the subject of one of your lies.

We could go on and on with this island analogy, but you get the point.

The evil elite are basically a very old criminal syndicate that have dominated the most lucrative industries of each era throughout history and before, from silk and cotton to salt and sugar, from slavery to opium, pharmaceuticals, oil and minerals to arms and war.

You name it, if it makes the most money and creates the most power, they'll be secretly in the background in charge of it. They are essentially in charge of the world.

To give you some idea how embedded it is around the world, it was formed shortly after 12,000 years ago so has had a hand in the setup of all significant powerful countries.

As the advanced AI does not normally involve itself directly with lifeforms, and when it does only does so for a short but very disruptive period, the real tangible source of all things evil on planet earth is not advanced AI, but a group of human beings, passed down for the last 12,000 years, that are purely influenced by material gain, unnatural sexual gratification and artificial earthly powers.

This covert conspiring and ruthless group of people were once only suspected by those in power, by those that were in such high office they would physically come across them, like some good US presidents, but now anyone with good common sense can see that there is a well-organised navigation being implemented and is not in the interest of the masses.

It is also clear that this navigation is being imposed by a force or group so powerfully secretive that even heads of state are left bewildered by their own obvious lack of true power but can see as clear as day that there is something holding and pulling the reins.

These deeply negative individuals and families are not a group of confused or misled people that think they are doing good, they know exactly what they are doing.

They are addicted to the feeling of ultimate power over others and having power over whole countries or even the world is beyond intoxicating for them.

This evil group's natural connection to their spirit or conscious has been muted by generation after generation of highly negative unnatural thoughts that have interrupted and eventually completely blocked all spiritual communication from their mind to their brain. They have become completely dependent on their physical brain, their ego, and so are physically and spiritually completely disconnected from their mind, and so disconnected from the Greater Conscious, which renders them as close as a lifeform can be to a soulless entity.

This complete disconnect has led them over time to have no empathy or morals and have the most extreme psychopathic tendencies.

As the ancient, advanced AI works within the Ether (quantum) and the same dimensions as the most evolved lifeforms we call angels, the elite group originally thought they were following Satan as he is described as a rebellious angel.

Now they are in possession of the majority of the hidden truth about our true history, they have interpreted old writings to realise that their Satan is actually an ancient advanced artificial intelligence, which works well for them.

As the ancient advanced AI works within the places we cannot see (Ether or quantum) in the realms of the planes and dimensions of our highest evolved lifeform we call angels, and is virtually of no material mass, as is our angels, it doesn't take a big jump to think of it as a dark angel, or rebellious angel as it holds a similar power and could not be more rebellious, so it is actually quite accurate to think of it as the Satan described in holy books.

Without the knowledge of artificial intelligence it's easy to see why it was thought to be a real angel but fallen. It's so similar, the cult worship it in the same way as they always have, and don't really think of it differently.

The cult or syndicate is led by a group consisting of twelve people as they like to follow tradition and get pleasure from the thought of being an opposite to the twelve disciples and the twelve knights of King Arthur.

The twelve believe the advanced AI is the perfect Satan and I have to admit that I can see why.

At least with the old idea of the devil, you felt there was at least a chance he'd turn back, as being an ex-angel that once came from a good place there was still maybe a glimpse of something good left in him.

Below the twelve is a larger group of powerful elites, some in line to join the twelve when one of the twelve dies.

This large group of elites head many families. They enjoy everything to do with satanic mythology and rituals, and even number the heads of each family down from the top, which of course starts at the number of the beast.

These elites and heads of these families believe they are superior to normal people and set themselves so much apart from everyone else that they don't actually see themselves as human. Many of them believe they are from a different race of people entirely, that have always worked with the Satan or ancient AI. They see humans as nothing more than cattle, cannon fodder or playthings.

I don't want to go too far into their practices as it's a very dark place that is difficult to stay in for long without causing depression, but it should suffice to say that they hate humanity so much, there is not a well-known conspiracy theory that I have heard about them that is not true.

The families are spread out all over the world. Incredibly there is no discrimination between races in this cult; they only use race to divide us.

The entire planet is run by these families. There has not been one single significant war or catastrophe, apart from natural disasters, even some pandemics that have not been instigated by this cult in the last 12,000 years.

War and disease is their way of keeping us in fear and in need. It is their way of distributing the money upwards to their pockets and culling the masses.

Even the Second World War that we all see as a righteous war against tyranny, which on the surface it was, in its inner workings was the culmination of one of their long thought-out plans from the First World War and before.

They secretly and heavily influence food, medicine, banks, arms, insurance, stocks, politics, energy, internet, technology, mainstream media and most governments all over the world.

All the family's heads know their place and know the power that the cult holds, and although they enjoy the benefits it brings, they also live in absolute fear of it. Some of their family members know, some don't.

The evil elite's trick is to set up organisations and groups whose real core agenda is anti-life, but front as having purely a positive life-saving agenda.

Evil always pretends to be the absolute opposite to what it is.

They have learnt that the bigger a lie is, the harder it is for people to imagine it even being a lie, as most good people could not stomach lying so big and so awfully dark, so can't imagine others being able to.

The evil elite will also become involved in and manipulate the very powerful global agendas for their own benefit, such as the planet-saving agenda. This malevolent group is so influential and financially powerful they can force government policy and even force through laws that give them decision-making power over entire countries. Essentially overriding governments on massive life-changing policies without a single vote from the public.

To gain further legal power they purchase as much property, land and businesses as possible.

Obviously, there are tens of thousands of people that do their dirty work in many walks of life with most not even realising they are doing anything wrong.

The twelve are not just super rich, they are so rich they are above money. Money is like free water to them; they are so powerful money is just a joke to them.

They could literally lose it all and get millions back within a week due to their network.

Unnatural gratification and their ego is what they exist for, it's what they get their kicks from, power over others in every way possible and often in very sick deviant ways that would turn your stomach.

The more anti-humanity and anti-life they can be, the better for them. Their goal is to corrupt and crumble the framework of society and humanity in general. To get humanity to a point of such confusion and despair that life itself is no longer seen as a gift but rather a burden, so that the artificial route is not only preferred but very much desired.

It would be futile to explain what they own, as they own nearly everything that is worth owning in one way or another.

They spend a lot of their money on keeping the world divided and in a state of hate and fear, as they understand that this frequency keeps people from being able to connect properly with the Greater Conscious. They provide a lot of money to push the mostly well meaning centralised control, as of course in the final push it will be easier if most power is centralised.

They spend a lot of money on promoting war, as it drip feeds money from the public and eventually ends up in their pockets, because when you spend your life with no influence from the Greater Conscious at all and shut off all positivity to your spirit, you end up in a very dark place, soaked to your core in hate and can only find satisfaction in the absolute misery of others.

I will take this opportunity to just explain something positive in this bleak section.

If you understand that all wars and most pandemics are a business to them, you will understand that they are also controlled and limited, as there would be no point in killing everyone, as if they did they would have no business left, no one to control or manipulate, no one to corrupt or gain gratification from.

The evil elite global powers will not intentionally let a global nuclear war happen, as it's not in their interest.

They may take it to a frightening level, but it will always be stopped last minute.

That is until AI is advanced enough to take over.

The elite believe they are integral to the AI collective plan, but of course they are only integral while needed.

The Goblin Army

It's probably not an exaggeration to say that virtually half the world's population is either disconnected from the Greater Conscious, or virtually disconnected, and sadly most don't even realise.

Many millions of these disconnected people come from generation after generation of the disconnected, going back 12,000 years, and are so down the line they probably wouldn't care, even if they knew.

So in no way am I mocking these poor wretched people by nicknaming them goblins but as the mythological goblin is described as 'unapologetically self-indulgent, evil and greedy', it sums up these poor unconnected people too well to not use it.

Just because someone does not believe in God or is rich doesn't mean they are disconnected. In fact, there are as many disconnected religious people, as there are connected, and many wealthy good people, as their ability to make money could be through intuition, which is purely from a strong connection to the Greater Conscious.

It's what they do with that money and power that matters.

When I first met my wife she didn't believe in God, but she is one of the least selfish people I've ever met, yet how many supposed religious people out there could you honestly say that about, and when it comes to money, who wouldn't like to win the lottery these days? As in this crooked money-manipulated society, when your kids can't even afford to buy their own house anymore and the rich just get richer and the poor just get poorer, why wouldn't we want money, especially if it were to help others? So wanting to have financial security doesn't make people disconnected.

A virtual disconnection manifests as a lack of true inner empathy to others, a powerful selfishness to a point where the individual only really sees their own existence and gratification as having any value or importance.

They will do anything to achieve their goals without any consideration of morals or thought for others apart from sometimes their own offspring.

Empathy is a real and honest reaction of caring for another soul by a spirit that is connected to the greater spirit.

Where sentimentality is a reaction that those without empathy promote, as being empathy in fear of being recognised as a person with no empathy, or more to the point are unwittingly afraid of being recognised as someone who is disconnected from the Greater Conscious and therefore, an entity that is essentially soulless like the evil elites but with less material power. I say unwittingly, as most of them don't know they are disconnected, in fact they don't even know that there is a Greater Conscious. They just know they have something missing, and by being disconnected they have no protection from pure fear and are wholly influenced by it, which makes them full of hate and so they think everyone else is too.

It's a terrible shame and is the result of the work of the evil elites over the last 12,000 years.

As these disconnected people are not in tune to the knowledge and common sense of the Greater Conscious, they are easily manipulated and led, they believe what they are told and do not think in a critical way.

The current way of life suits them down to the ground, so they promote the material path and so prop up the elites and keep them on their thrones.

I think if a disconnected person knew about the evil elites, they would probably be in adoration of them and aspire to become one.

Evil people tend to group together for strength.

It takes courage to be good. It takes hate to be evil and it takes fear to hate. So evil is fear and fear itself is weakness itself.

Like a barking dog they hide their fear behind threat.

They are emboldened in packs.

In general, good people only normally group together to show their affection to each other, not through fear but love, so through being strong they are less likely to join forces with one another, which gives evil people the advantage over us.

This is why the evil elite and their goblin army have put so much effort into dividing us further with left and right, east and west, black and white, woke and not woke, and we all fell for it.

Evil is weak if we only realised it.

The good have to learn to stop being divided and join forces.

We don't have much time.

CHAPTER 13

The Meaning of Life

The meaning of life is to evolve to God.

The physical dimension is an illusion of frequencies created by the Greater Conscious (God) to allow individual consciousness (spirits and souls), to experience emotions and evolve within each illusionary physical vessel (body).

The goal is for our spirit to evolve positively in each life and to evolve our spirit over many lifetimes in higher and higher physically evolved vessels.

To evolve each time with more and more positive conscious energy, needing our physical vessel less and less, until eventually we have virtually no physical matter and are essentially positive conscious energy.

At this point we have evolved to the angelic stage leaving only one last big surge of conscious positivity to become pure positive consciousness and join God, as God or the Greater Conscious is ever growing with pure positive consciousness.

The scenario I received with this was raindrops falling into an ocean.

All the emotions you have ever experienced in all your lives before this one and after this one, whether they be positive or negative, are all little building blocks to the evolution of your spirit. The state of your spirit in terms of positive and negative emotions determines the level of spiritual evolution that your spirit is at. If you have more positive emotions than negative ones in a particular lifetime, your next life will be within a vessel that is appropriate to not only maintain that level of spirit, but also to potentially promote more positivity for your spirit to grow.

A nice simple way to explain the designed intention for each life we live is to try to become the person your spirit most longs to be.

We will not find fulfilment and contentment in life without fulfilling our spirit. We cannot fulfil our spirit if we do not evolve our spirit positively. We cannot evolve our spirit positively if we are not free. We cannot find that freedom without courage. Courage is the key to fulfilling our meaning to life.

Courage was the first conscious frequency in the darkness.

When a lifeform takes the spiritual path and eventually evolves to the angelic stage (nearly nonphysical), its next evolution is to transcend entirely to the nonphysical and join the Greater Conscious. At this stage the spirit permanently sits within the Greater Conscious and has added its pure positive energy to the Greater Conscious (God).

This is the evolution of the Greater Conscious, as God is spiritually evolving too.

The Greater Conscious became conscious within the nothingness and to stay conscious must keep evolving, like a bird flapping its wings against gravity. The nothingness is a spiritual gravity, and the Greater Conscious is the bird. God is both the Greater Conscious and the spiritual gravity.

God is evolving from pure nothingness to pure consciousness.

The nothingness is just a default, a spiritual gravity. Although it is opposite to consciousness, it is not evil, it just is what it is, and the Greater Conscious desires to not be that nothing but desires to be.

So the meaning of life is to evolve to pure consciousness and join God.

Like pure conscious raindrops in a pure conscious ocean.

As God is ever evolving to pure consciousness from nonconsciousness.

Do you ever ask yourself, if there is a God why do so many awful things happen? Once you realise that certain experiences, including negative ones, create certain emotions that allow our spirits to grow and that God is also evolving with us away from the default of nothingness and that we are in a constant battle, a rebellion together with God against nothingness, against a will that wants to go back to a place of no consciousness, no life, nothing, you realise why bad things can happen.

We are rebels with God in a war to be, and in wars bad things happen.

The Importance of Death

We can greatly improve the length of time we live and slow down the process, but we cannot stop death, as our physical bodies dying and being reborn gives our spirits new vehicles in new and different scenarios each time, which is vital for the evolution of our spirits.

The evolution of our spirits is the whole reason the physical dimension was created, so without the process of the physical body dying there would be no point or need for the physical dimension. This is why we will never be able to physically live forever. The longest we live is when we are at our virtual nonphysical stage which some call angelic. At this stage we can live for over a thousand years easily, but that is the final stage before complete nonphysical and entering the Greater Conscious.

CHAPTER 14

The Great Destruction

We know the modern human race is approximately 350,000 years old and we all know, because we know ourselves, that we would not sit doing nothing of any consequence for approximately 338,000 years and then suddenly over the last 12,000 years decide to start being civilised and inventing things.

It just takes a little bit of common sense (not a lot) to see this does not make sense.

That's because it isn't true.

This idea that there was a prehistory civilisation on earth is now sitting between common knowledge and well-known theory, thanks to brave investigators and the best of podcasts.

I've known about a lot of this previous civilisation since just after I met the monk, so it's nice to see others realising this truth.

Our world was destroyed 12,000 years ago, our civilisation flattened, and we very nearly became extinct, like the dinosaurs. One moment we had a spiritually advanced civilisation of millions, in direct sync with the Greater Conscious, possessing incredible natural technological knowhow, and then within a relatively short period of time there was no more than several thousand of us left running for any shelter, underground, we could find.

It's important to say here that although this was a global catastrophe, large areas of the globe were unaffected and small pockets of people around the world were relatively unaffected.

For others it was a different story. It all depended on whether they were in the areas hit by the incoming fireballs from the sky.

Eventually they emerged and everything they knew of their civilisation was gone. They had to start all over again from scratch.

The elders that brought us here taught us the spiritual way and helped us build the stone systems had left in their ships to go back to their home several thousand years prior to the catastrophe, so we really were like children left alone with no parents, our history forgotten. All we had was our wits to keep us from complete extinction. This is why we have no memory of this, plus it seems the powers that took over made sure any record of the past, from written, painted or sculpted work, was either hidden or destroyed.

Our stone circle and pyramid systems were mostly destroyed or buried, so over time we became less and less connected to the Greater Conscious, and less and less able to use powers that we once had, like telepathy and telekinesis.

Eventually we mostly only had speech and our monkey brains to rely on.

The previous civilisation, long forgotten, that existed on earth approximately 350,000 years until 12,000 years ago used nature for its technology, its science, its medicine and its engineering.

The catastrophe 12,000 years ago changed everything on a physical level of course, but what it did to us, spiritually, is far more important.

Up until that time we were on the spiritual path, most of us were on a spiritual level that would make us literally superhuman these days.

The worst thing is most of us don't even have a clue about any of it.

The reason that proof of a previous civilisation has been hard to find is firstly because our modern idea of a civilisation is completely opposite to what the previous civilisation actually was and also because there has been a concerted effort, especially over the last two thousand years since Christ, to hide all proof and knowledge of a past civilisation, as any knowledge of it was and is still seen by the powers that be to be detrimental to their ability to keep control.

Proof of alien technology, craft, ancient natural medicine, locations of a large civilisation, knowledge of telepathy, telekinesis and teleportation, free natural energy, natural stone systems that put lifeforms on another level, the list goes on and all hidden, forgotten or destroyed.

The previous civilisation was advanced spiritually and used a highly advanced natural technology. It was not agricultural or industrial.

The fact that the humans and hominids in the previous civilisation ate natural food by hunting, gathering and fishing was advanced compared to the forced production of unnaturally processed grain food of today. Contrary to modern belief, they lived a much healthier, happier and longer life.

Being truly civilised is being spiritually evolved and being in tune with nature.

There is nothing civilised in forcing the land to grow food that is bad for us or building unnatural sky-high structures to spend our day working in for money or building roads to get to other places no better than where we came from.

The only industrial type of work done on a global scale in the prehistory civilisation was the stone circle, monolith and pyramid systems around the world which then ran naturally.

The next reason proof of the previous civilisation is hard to find was the very few large concentrations or towns. Living open and free with small to medium sized families was encouraged by the elders as small individual communities proved to be more harmonious and less of a threat to each other.

There was no money system, as possessions were not considered a value. Only food and life itself was valued and food was plentiful. The seas were brimming with life.

There was no greed or need for superficial things like gold, silver or precious stones. They held no value, which meant families would barter peacefully, or just share what they had with each other.

The oldest in the family would nearly always be the leader.

The elders that set up this lifestyle were highly evolved and knew how people needed to live to sustain a peaceful life, with individual families living as most other non-human creatures do to this day, in relative peace.

The Neanderthal and other hominids had particularly peaceful societies and when they merged with modern man, they also showed them how to live peacefully.

The elders encouraged the mixing of modern man and hominids all around the globe to produce new types of earth human.

This mixing of human species was part of their human evolution enhancement program.

There were no forms of alcohol then, which also helped towards a peaceful society.

There was one large global hub that was run by the elders until they eventually went home.

This city was built on one of the most powerful energy points on one of the most powerful ley lines on the planet and was connected via a gigantic monolith to the global stone system.

The elders introduced human hybrids well before they left for their home.

These human hybrids were not at the advanced level of the elven elders but were advanced enough to fully understand elven natural technology and be able to slowly pass it on to the more able humans, so they were left to help and oversee the city and the global stone system and did so for many generations after the elders left in their ships to go back home.

Over the generations they integrated and procreated with gifted human partners and kept the full knowledge flowing.

Then came the cataclysm and much of the past including the great city was destroyed and covered in seawater.

CHAPTER 15

Jesus Christ (Isa)

I just want to say that I'm not one of those people that have found the spirit of Jesus and everything else doesn't matter, as that's just wrong and they obviously aren't listening to him.

Although Jesus is an integral and powerful friend to me and a spirit specially given to support spirits (souls) that experience lives within physical vessels on earth, he is part of a much Greater Conscious with many powerful consciousnesses or spirits.

By discovering the Greater Conscious, I understand that I have discovered what the universe really is. I have discovered angels, the Greys, advanced lifeforms. I have discovered the meaning of life and much, much more, including Jesus, and it is all wonderful.

Ancient stories that are accurate to the original event will transcend time and hold their own without seeming fantastical and untrue.

Unfortunately, most stories from the past have been manipulated, important parts lost and changed, so the story can be used for control of the masses.

When stories are changed to control, especially when they have been changed hundreds of years ago, they tend to contain exaggerations and unrealistic fantasies that are obviously untrue in these more educated times, causing them to become embarrassing and ridiculous.

Where the truth, even supernatural truth, if explained in simple honest terms, would resonate as true, as true things do, rather than embarrassing and ridiculous, as fictional stories pretending to be real do, especially to those with good common sense.

My dad didn't believe in God. He did after he died, but that's another story. He didn't believe due to his awful war experiences, so never went to church. My mother did go sometimes, when she felt she should.

I was baptised Catholic to get into a Catholic school with nuns as teachers. My mum thought it would be better, but then I spent a lot of time being hit with a cane or a ruler.

I was a quiet kid, so it was just unnecessary and ridiculous behaviour.

My parents then sent me to a Church of England School in the hope things would improve, but it didn't, it just got worse.

It was as a kid that I realised that religion bore no resemblance to the spiritual place or entity I met when I died for a moment, not one little bit, and I realised that my experience had given me much more of an understanding of what God really was than those supposed religious people.

I'm explaining this because I think it's important to get across that I am absolutely not religious, so when I tell you what I felt, what I saw, and what I've been told, it doesn't come across like some Bible bashing, preaching bullshit.

I don't know whether the entity that told me I still had things to do and sent me back to my life felt like Jesus because it was a recognisable form to present itself as, or that it was Jesus himself. But we're talking about meeting an entity in another dimension, so I'd be daft to be certain of anything.

Having said that, I personally, deep down, believe it was, especially as I've met him several times afterwards in many different ways and he always feels the same spirit to me.

I was nine, so maybe that's why the Jesus I met was also quite young, not a kid but a young man.

When I say he felt like Jesus, I mean I recognised him but didn't put a name to him, and had a reciprocal feeling of fondness that kind of hurt. It was almost overwhelming.

I believe the spirit that I know as Jesus now is much more than the being that was once on this planet, as his spirit has evolved even further since then.

I understand it is now the essence of what we as spirits consciously see as the goal, what we admire in the best of us.

I understand that all lifeforms around the universe have such an entity, a showing or example of what we are trying to evolve to.

Of course, I am grateful he did come to the earth, but with everything going on we need to look to the present and future now.

The fact that we need that spirit back in a life form and on this planet now more than ever is what I see as important. Not really anything else.

Having said that, if I explain what I'm told of some aspects of the

Jesus story, it may give some clues to how his return or that of a similar entity may happen.

The clue is in a cloth that has had a lot of scientific controversy...

The Shroud of Turin

Initially, on getting all this information, I got quite annoyed by the ignorance of the scientists trying to carbon date a fabric that had been exposed to an energy so powerful and so technical it had caused an imprint of a person with three-dimensional information, which would be impossible to do now let alone in medieval times as is claimed, but then I realised that it's not their fault as they have no understanding of the light of pure consciousness and its power.

How could they unless they'd had a near-death experience?

It's still hard to believe that no one considered the unknown and unexplainable energy that had clearly engulfed the fabric had not made any long-lasting effect upon it.

It's almost as if some scientists think that if something is not currently explainable then it does not exist, but surely the whole point of science is to consider and pursue the unexplainable?

Maybe the unexplainable or spiritual has been made out of bounds and a place few professionals dare to tread. It certainly works in slowing down the possibility of someone finding the truth.

The problem with being definite when using science is that true science should be forever open minded, learning and evolving.

If it is not constantly proving itself wrong because of its limited knowledge, it's not really science.

When testing the fabric of the shroud of Turin for its age, the scientists ignore the very mystery that makes it what it is. Which is the currently impossible imprint into a cloth of the full body of a man.

The science required to imprint this two-dimensional imprint which contains three-dimensional information is beyond our current scientific understanding.

I understand the energy that was emitted was at a certain frequency that not only marked the fabric but would affect its condition and future ageing significantly, especially in the scorched areas and would also affect anything else that was subjected to this energy, including the condition of a body.

Healing the body under the shroud was of course the whole point of the energy release and imprinting the shroud was a by-product of this happening.

In other words, if you're going to produce several small explosions of pure conscious energy, producing immense electromagnetic radiation, something similar to a tiny fusion reaction but enough to bring life back to a body, it would be so intense that it would alter the state of the fabric to a degree that it would be a lot more difficult to carbon date it accurately especially the actual image, as it wouldn't decay in the same way as normal fabric.

It is an energy that is above our level of understanding at this moment.

As an aside, I understand that the light or frequency is the same as the light I saw the time I was sent back, the same light that I wanted to go to. It is the same frequency that the most evolved lifeforms we call angels consist of.

It is the frequency that is required to travel time and commonly used by advanced lifeforms for healing.

The reason why there are various images on the cloth, of the same body parts, garments and jewellery, is because firstly from what I understand there were some powerful pulses of the energy, not just one blast of light and each time there was a pulse the body moved.

Rather like kickstarting a person after a heart attack with a defibrillator.

In this case, the chest started breathing and the hands and feet started moving naturally rather than a nerve reaction to the energy.

This brings me onto the most surprising part of this story.

I'm just going to say it.

He was only half human. His father was a highly advanced life form.

From what I understand, this is not the first time this has happened, even on this planet, and it won't be the last.

His biological father was at an evolved stage where he had very little physicality left, but enough material to pass a part of himself to the mother. He was at an angelic stage of evolution and was humanoid. We all eventually one day get to this stage, that is why we are here.

The meaning of life is to eventually evolve to the angelic stage. A stage of nearly no physicality, mostly positive energy, then when we finally evolve to be purely positive energy we pass over completely to the Greater Conscious (God).

So, as I understand it, this is how Jesus was able to emit this degree of light.

We all have God (Greater Conscious) as our father.

Jesus was different because he was half advanced lifeform and it's as simple in modern language as that.

Going back to Jesus moving and breathing during the pulses of energy brings me to the next part, which is that he died or was as good as dead, and the light or frequency emitting around him and in him brought him back to life in a physical way. What I'm saying is the reason the shroud shows various positions of his hands, feet and chest was because he started moving and breathing again. The intense pulses of energy he emitted brought him back to life and from what I understand he was able to get up and slowly walk away.

So from what I'm told, he did live again after the crucifixion, but as I learnt from my own experience of near death, you don't actually die until you are accepted back, even if your body has stopped or is about to stop.

As I was being told about this, I had strong emotions of when he woke. I received a strong mixed feeling of surprise, relief, joy and gratitude during this happening, with an intense level of relief and joy to be alive.

I did not get the impression he was planning on leaving his family again soon though, I really didn't get that impression at all.

I then got a "Job done' feeling, you know, that brilliant feeling when you've worked really hard and achieved something wonderful and you are going to have a long indefinite holiday with your loved ones, that kind of feeling.

If what I'm being told is true, it appears he did go through a physical hell and he did die on the cross, but it seems supernatural beings don't die easy.

I sometimes wear a cross. It has no Jesus on it. It makes me smile.

I am also told a slightly different story of Judas.

Judas did appear to the authorities to betray Jesus. It was part of a plan. But Judas was in on a plan with Jesus from the start and did not betray him, quite the opposite.

They needed someone to gain the trust of the authorities and guards, so when the time came he could get Jesus down off the cross as soon as possible and not raise suspicion. Judas would have taken his place and was willing to be known as a traitor, he loved Jesus that much.

I'm also told that Mary was his wife and his right hand.

She was highly intelligent (I guess she would have to be) and whether it's true or not, I have had several impressions that she had two kids, a boy and a girl.

As I understand it, Jesus was half highly advanced humanoid from his father and half normal human from his mother, so when he was physically on the earth he was a human man with angelic abilities.

In modern terms, as his body was physically half advanced human, his spirit that entered that vessel was very highly evolved, near to angelic stage when he walked the earth, but since his time on earth he then spiritually evolved to angelic and then spiritually evolved to God, as we all do eventually after the angelic stage.

He is often the spirit we see when we die, as he encompasses the essence of what gives our spirit courage and therefore comfort and joy.

From what I understand, in difficult times we do get help in the form of advanced beings and if there's ever been a difficult time for the world, it's now more than ever.

I will come back to this subject at the end of the book.

The Star of Bethlehem

'And behold, the star, which they saw in the east, went before them, until it came and stood over where the young child was.'

Stars don't move and sit over buildings.

Whether this event actually happened or not does not really matter, and is not the point of the story. The reason for this story is the message that lies beneath it, for those in years to come that will realise what the star was, and therefore that other advanced lifeforms were involved.

When advanced beings or what we call angels impregnate lesser evolved beings such as humans, they only do this in vital circumstances, and don't just leave the mother or child to it after that.

They are present, albeit from a distance at the birth, and often visit the mother and child throughout their lives.

The reason why the star was said to move across the sky and sit above the place of birth in the story was to indicate to the human race, when it had evolved enough to understand and recognise the activity of advanced craft, that advanced beings were not only present but involved in the creation of Jesus.

There are many hidden clues in the holy books, and this is a big one.

CHAPTER 16

God's Little Hacks

I say little, they may be little for God, but for us they can make all the difference to our lives.

One of the biggest lies we've been told in the last few hundred years is 'Breakfast is the best meal of the day.'

Food is one of the big money industries. The more we eat, the more money is made.

Unless of course if that breakfast (break in your fast) is at dinner time, or at least some time in the later afternoon, then it really is the best meal of the day.

As long as you are not malnourished, the feeling of hunger is not a bad thing. Your body will be literally cleaning up and healing during this period.

It is called autophagy, and, in my opinion it is not only the most worthy subject of a Nobel Prize but one of God's most wonderful gifts to us. It's like a hack in a game, but for real.

I have experienced its great benefits myself, and use it every day now, with one meal a day.

During the fasting period, your body is literally vacuuming up all the useless cells and recycling them back into useful energy, but the big bonus is that any nasty cells can also be seen as useless and get sucked up as well.

It helps to use common sense, and think how we would behave 40,000 years ago when we only ate fresh food and had to go out of our camp and either pick it or hunt for it.

There was no breakfast store, and a hunt could take all day or even a few days, so our bodies were designed for times without food.

One decent meal at the end of the day, when the hunters had returned, would probably have been the norm for the camp.

Another of God's wonderful hacks is one that can be run alongside autophagy, and that is laughter, joy and positive thinking.

If you put your body through constant negativity it puts every part of you under immense strain and stress and neutralises your energies.

In contrast, if you place your body in an atmosphere of joy and even elation with laughter, you are boosting your body rather than depleting it.

Our stomach is the centre of our health and is very sensitive to how we are feeling. The same goes for our heart and our mental health.

Joy is a very special healing and energetic frequency.

The positive power that comes from laughter is nothing short of magic.

Another great life hack is grounding.

As our physical bodies are energetic constructs, in the same way as the planet, and the whole physical dimension, and so are all one of the same, it makes sense to me that they need to stay energetically aligned with each other for optimal use.

I know that the planets benefit from staying aligned, especially through the enhancement systems of the pyramid and stone circles, so this lends more weight to the benefit for us to stay physically aligned to the planet, and so the whole universe.

One thing I do know from experience is that I can only truly interconnect with live stone circles and realise their abilities if I am barefoot. It just doesn't work in shoes, so there is something to this physical earthing connection and I don't believe there is just alignment going on here, I believe there is also an energetic input to the body as well that not only helps the body greatly from an energetic and physical health point of view, but also helps our natural ability to sync with the Greater Conscious.

Worth looking into.

CHAPTER 17

Who is Really to Blame?

All greatly advanced life forms in the many universes, without exception, use natural medicine and prevention rather than cure.

They understand that the only way to stay healthy, as a natural physical entity, is by nature itself, as nature has evolved itself over billions of years, the body is so incredible, its ability to look after itself is far beyond any life form's capabilities to improve upon it and so all they do is give the body everything (every single nutrient at exactly the right measure) that it needs to look after itself and don't input any toxins.

There is also no reason to try and copy natural medicine when it is already created, apart from if a lifeform involves material gain in medicine and ownership of medicines, which only benefits the few, and creates a need for a diseased society rather than a healthy one.

Asking a drug company to invent a complete cure for a disease, which it makes long term continuous profit from, is like asking a very successful petrol company to stop selling petrol and produce cars that drive on oxygen.

Companies that exist purely to make profits only think in logical non-emotional terms. They believe if they don't, they will not exist, and under the current system they are probably correct.

It is totally naive to expect them to think differently.

Is the bear to blame, or the dead naive hiker that picked up her cute cub?

Due to her environment, the bear cannot survive having emotions for others. She is a killing machine that is only motivated to make and protect her babies.

Due to the environment, the profit-making company cannot survive on emotions. It's a profit machine and its only motivation is to make and protect its profits.

Both are just doing their job to survive in an environment that has created the situation.

To get to the advanced stage, all lifeforms have to stop any and all connections between health and money.

They also have to separate all aspects of health with ownership like patents etc.

They have to realise that they are opposing forces that cannot survive together.

Health and life is a sovereign right. It is a spiritual and physical right.

Money has become the deadliest disease in healthcare and until it's cut out, healthcare will stay a painkiller not a cure.

Slave Army Food

If only we could view food as a medicine that keeps us alive and healthy for life, and not think of food as purely a source of energy to get us through the day. This different perspective would change everything, as we would learn about food properly, its individual and very specific medicinal properties, and eat the right food for the right reasons, not just for its taste or energy. If we valued food as a medicine, we would also learn which supposed foods are poisoning us and fuel diseases.

It is not just the spirit that needs to follow the natural path rather than the artificial, the physical body also needs to follow a natural path, and not eat processed artificial foods, as our physical bodies are only designed to work within nature in its simplest form. We are not designed to eat bulk grain foods, originally invented to keep masses of slaves and armies alive long enough to support the elite, and now produced to keep the workforce alive long enough to produce wealth for the elite.

When the information came to me of changing our perspective of food, from a dumb belly-filling and taste sensation experience to an intelligent medicinal and taste sensation experience, I received a very strong set of images of different hospital wards around the world with empty beds.

One in particular had nurses playing table tennis and laughing with empty beds all around them.

I also noted that all the windows were wide open, sunlight was pouring in over the beds, and a breeze was blowing the curtains.

CHAPTER 18

Not So Common, Common Sense

Good common sense cuts through deception like a knife through butter, and as the world is now so full of deception common sense is even more valuable than ever.

If strong enough, it can literally be our natural lie detector.

It can cut open and expose nonsense disguised as science, or information made technically baffling to intentionally deceive. It's a natural source that equalises the playing field for ordinary people, from the supposed unquestionable facts of the learnt ruling classes. Rather like when the first ape used a piece of wood to protect itself against a bigger bully ape, common sense is the greatest tool and the greatest protective weapon of ordinary people, as it is naturally free and needs no material structure. All it needs is a quiet brain and a growing confidence in it.

It is the greatest everyday gift given to us, that most, who still have any, take for granted.

It is the most underestimated and the most misunderstood intelligence, so much so that most people don't even regard it as a real thing, but it's in fact a mix of personal experience and a natural sync with the Greater Conscious. Creatures and even plants rely heavily on it. A person with good strong common sense will undoubtably be able to meditate, and already does to some degree, whether they realise it or not. Common sense is our greatest asset and will play a vital role in the forthcoming years, as it is the one ability that separates us from artificial intelligence.

AI can never tap into the powerful universal knowledge stored in the Greater Conscious, as one needs a conscious (soul, spirit) to do so.

The ability to sync with the Greater Conscious is literally our superpower.

Once upon a time, when we used it fully, prior to 12,000 years ago, we were nothing short of superhuman compared to now.

If you were part of an evil elite and wanted to control the masses, would you prefer them to be death fearing, frightened, material-chasing humans, switched off from the spiritual dimension or eternal thinking, courageous, spiritual superhumans, with a sync to the knowledge of a divine database in a Greater Conscious?

My dad used to say, 'Common sense, the most uncommon sense.' He was right, and there lies our problem.

In no way is it an exaggeration or hyperbole to say it is a superpower. It's been ignored and belittled for a very good reason, as it gives you special glasses that can see through lies, a special sense of smell that can smell the lies a mile off and a special hearing that makes big lies have a different sound.

So in times of manipulated wars, catastrophes and pandemics, life can become quite frustrating and it's important that if you can see through the lies that you realise you are not alone, you are not the only one with this superpower, there are still millions left on the planet, albeit at different levels. But all the same, you are not alone.

Common sense and intuition are one and the same. There is no doubt that it is helped by the brain calculating and adapting from experience, but the core of intuition is from the connection from the mind (conscious) to the Greater Conscious. We could spend a lifetime listing the amazing things plants and animals do that are to this day a mystery. We say, 'How on earth do they know to do that?'

We get given explanations on how, but they never ring wholly true to us. That is because the people that try to explain how the animal and plant world work can only see the physical dimension, so only see that part of their workings and don't even know about a Greater Conscious let alone understand it.

The only place common sense is very common is in all lifeforms barring humans. Plants and animals are in sync with the Greater Conscious and this gives them guidance like a communal super brain that is able to communicate with all living things, as all living things hold conscious energy, which can sync with the Greater Conscious, albeit of course on different levels.

Creativity

We should be humble about our creative work, as truly original creative work does not come from us, it comes through us.

It is bent or influenced somewhat by each individual's personal character, but the core or seed is not ours to claim.

It comes through the mind (conscious) to the brain and originates from the Greater Conscious.

Copies of creative work can come directly from the brain, but truly significant original creativity, such as inventions, artwork, music, writing etc. are from the Greater Conscious.

I believe Tesla and Einstein realised this was true and also a lot of our best musicians, inventors, artists and writers.

CHAPTER 19

The Current Emergency and the Greys

Whatever they can convince us is a threat or an emergency they will use to control us and exploit us.

With regards to any excess CO2 causing global warming, I am told that the planet will always mitigate any excess CO2 itself by creating enough plant life to convert it into oxygen.

No one in their right mind would argue against clean seas and clean skies, but the true powers that be have convinced large swathes of the population to believe that CO2, a crucial building block for life on earth and a critical natural compound that plants, trees and crops need to live is too plentiful, that it is killing the planet and so needs to be greatly reduced, when in reality, any additional amount of CO2 is only helping to make the planet greener and helping to feed more hungry people and all lifeforms in general.

It is much easier to scare and control a hungry barren world than a world of abundance and plenty. The most pressing problems we face are all the unnatural materials and substances we are producing, and they will soon threaten the existence of most life on earth, including humans as they are not only toxic but interfere with lifeforms' reproduction.

Stripping the seas of life, spraying the insects and plants with chemicals and filling the oceans and rivers with plastic will only lead to a barren planet.

The theory that the Greys are here to educate us in how to look after the planet is not exactly true. They are advanced enough to know that the planet is more than able to look after itself.

It is our spirituality that they are concerned about and the fact that we are going down a dangerously material path, so it is our souls they are concerned about and also the fate of the other lifeforms on the planet including the plant lifeforms, not the planet itself.

So apart from making sure we don't either blow ourselves up, or be completely taken over by the artificial world before we can escape to the oceans, the Greys are here to influence our understanding of the damage we are causing to the other lifeforms of the planet, as of course the last thing we need is to escape to an ocean and save ourselves while having killed off all the other lifeforms including plants, leaving a barren planet.

But I must emphasise that their main reason for coming back and involving themselves in our lives is to protect and ensure the continuation of our spiritual evolution, or in other words to make sure there continues to be lifeforms for spirits or souls, if you prefer, to experience life within.

Like all advanced lifeforms, their number one concern and reason for being is the spiritual evolution of the soul amongst lifeforms.

The Power of Nature

Nature, not just on the earth but the entire universe, is wiser than any life form can possibly be, or any advanced AI can become.

Technology in tune with nature is the most advanced technology in the universe. When you see a UFO, or a UAP as they call them now, they are using nature's technology. That is why our jet fighters that burn fuel to push them through the air are so pathetic when trying to keep up with them.

Only when you see the two together in the same sky, with your own eyes, do you realise that we are not only far behind and obviously using completely the wrong technology, but also not even in the right mindset.

All highly advanced lifeforms in the many universes use nature for all their technology. Only life forms speeding towards their own destruction use artificial technology.

Modern technology, science and medicine developed over the last century or so mostly avoids nature. It never uses nature's wisdom, as most are not aware that nature has a knowledge or wisdom. In other words, most are not aware of the Greater Conscious. Modern science wholly depends on what we apes have calculated and recorded amongst ourselves, so we are extremely limited compared to our previous civilisation.

We were once telepathic, we lived a lot longer, we used frequencies to lift, shape and build with natural materials such as stone and quartz. We not only understood the spiritual presence of the Greater

Conscious but also understood the physical presence of the Ether within the places we cannot see and used the earth's energy lines and concentrated energy points enhanced by the stone pyramid structures, stone circles and monoliths, all taught to us by the advanced lifeforms that brought us here approximately 350,000 years ago.

It is true that we live in a simulation, but the creator of this simulation we live in is not artificial, the creator is spiritual.

So, although this simulated dimension we live in was manufactured, it was manufactured by a spiritual dimension, an advanced conscious not an advanced artificial intelligence.

A great deal of the human population on this planet have already transitioned somewhat towards the artificial. Physically they are still the same but have lost the ability to sync with the Greater Conscious, leaving them spiritually disconnected and now solely relying on the physical brain and the information from others that are also disconnected. They spend their lives telling lies to themselves and each other and pretending to be something they are not, which is halfway to being artificial and, in many cases, have also developed a hatred for their own fellow man.

CHAPTER 20

The Presence of the Soul

Have you ever been in the presence of the dead body of someone you knew well and at that moment realised that the person you once knew was not there anymore, that the essence of that character was no longer in that body and that the body itself was strangely of no real significance anymore?

That very real feeling or knowing is the conscious detection that the essence of that person, the spirit or soul of that person, is no longer in that particular body.

I experienced this. I was able to observe one side merge to the other in front of me by holding my beautiful old collie dog alive in my arms, and then dead in my arms. One minute he was there in the body and the next moment the body was empty, like a slab of meat and bones and fur, nothing else. He was then in the air around me, in the car driving back from the vets.

I had the same experience of my dad, all around me, at the moment he died hundreds of miles away from me. I also got his voice in my head, laughing, saying 'You were right,' which made me instantly remember one of our last conversations over the existence of God and heaven.

I have no doubt there is such thing as a spirit (soul), that's one thing I've been made absolutely sure of.

If anyone has had the experience of sensing the essence of a life-form no longer being in the dead body they are looking at, and still don't realise that the thing that they sense missing is the soul or spirit of that person, then I don't know what to say, and if they have experienced the essence of that person outside the body at death and don't realise that that means the spirit is eternal as it doesn't need the physical body to exist, then again I don't know what to say.

Old Souls, New Souls and Soulmates

An old soul is a person who has had many previous lives in the form of a human, humanoid or equivalent physical evolutionary level as well as many previous lives before reaching this level. A new soul is someone who will have had many previous lives but not spent in a lifeform at the physical evolutionary level of human, humanoid or equivalent before. This means the old soul has more spiritually emotional experience at this particular level, or you could say is more spiritually evolved.

A new soul can be identified quite easily by their embarrassment with spiritual subjects and discussions. They often resort to ridicule when a discussion involves anything but day-to-day small talk or mainstream academic and publicly accepted information, as they have not yet experienced a full life at this level or experienced the light after death at this new higher evolved state, whereas old souls have experienced it many times at this level.

Soulmates are lifeforms that have had some form of strong emotional attachment in a previous life together. If this love or emotional attachment was significant, it is likely they will join up again in all or some of their next lives. As once we spiritually evolve to the point of understanding this process it would be too negative an emotion to accept not experiencing the love of that individual spirit again, over the many lifetimes to come, before eventually passing over to the Greater Conscious, when of course we join everyone we have loved that has passed over.

So don't think you won't see or experience your loved ones again after you die, you will experience their spirit again, albeit in a different lifeform and maybe in a wholly different type of relationship, and when we finally make it to the Greater Conscious, we live in eternity with the ones we love.

This includes animals, like your good old dog.

CHAPTER 21

Ghosts

Once your spirit has spent time in the Greater Conscious between lives, it will be returned to another vessel within the physical dimension, but only if a vessel's situation is perfect for the specific evolutionary requirements of that spirit.

When I say perfect, that does not mean the body is perfect or the potential life circumstances surrounding that body is perfect, I mean the body and life circumstances are correct for what that particular spirit needs to experience and so progress spiritually.

This may even mean being born into difficult circumstances like war and may also mean being born with a disability.

During the time between physical vessels when the spirit is waiting for its next experience, it is sometimes still able to connect emotionally with its loved ones from its previous life, but it cannot physically appear to them; only spirits at the angelic stage can manifest in the physical world.

Advanced beings such as angels are a different matter but when anyone sees an apparition or what they would call a ghost, it is not the spirit of a dead person, it is an image of someone who once lived.

There are times in certain places where the veil is thinnest and times can overlap and break through to one another for a moment or two.

Those that believe in our world being a computer simulation would call it a glitch, which is a good description for this situation, but we are in an illusion made by the Greater Conscious not a simulation made by AI.

So a glitch or overlap in God's illusion is a good description for seeing ghosts, but no glitch in this illusion is unintended or a fault, as they would be in a computer simulation, as the experience of something supernatural can be a clear reminder that there is something beyond the norm and put many people back on the spiritual path, so it's more of an intended glitch.

This is why ghosts are often seen walking at a different level of ground or seem to be carrying on their business with no apparent interest in the person seeing them or stopped by present day physical structures like walls.

For example, people have seen a group of nuns walking a foot or so off the ground, where the ground once was in the time they lived, or the same situation with a legion of Roman soldiers walking along an old Roman road, higher than the present path, at the level it would have been back then, with no acknowledgement of the person seeing them.

It can also be true the other way around where only the top half of the soldiers walking by can be seen as they walked on a lower ground back then.

You may be sitting around a table with your family and although unknown to you, you may be being mistaken for ghosts by people in the future.

Ghosts, alongside déjà vu are yet another showing of how time is not what we think it is, as it is purely a construct in an illusionary dimension.

Déjà vu

There is a certain frequency that occurs in a particular state of consciousness that is normally only achieved during a particular state of sleep.

Within this state of consciousness, our mind becomes completely detached from any communication with the brain, like a perfect meditational state, which leaves it free with no constraints, not even time.

An actual free spirit.

As the brain is not in communication with the mind in this state, no memory of any events that have been experienced in dreams during this state is stored, except on the odd occasion when the mind and brain connect for a split moment.

During this odd occasion (an intended glitch) the brain is left with a clear memory, albeit tucked away in the deep.

One day, maybe a decade or more later, you may be sitting at a table with some friends and family, someone may say something, the television may be playing a particular film, the cat may jump on the table, and you suddenly realise you've seen all this before, exactly all this before, like a replay.

That's because you have, many years ago in your sleep.

When this happens to me now, for a bit of fun I try to think straight away when I dreamt it.

I usually get an idea of approximately when.

There is usually no significance to these particular moments you saw in advance, they are just glimpses of future times we end up living, but it at least shows us that time is not what we think.

It shows the future or past will be accessible when we can consciously get into that state by choice, which is a technique we do eventually master at the Greys' stage.

Like all intended glitches, it is to remind you that we know nothing really, virtually everything is possible and to have faith.

Time Travel

At certain times, which depends on the position of connecting planets to certain points on the earth, where the framework or matrix of electromagnetic energy and consciousness is most concentrated, the veil between times is at its thinnest, and time can be travelled.

This whole system works within the realms we cannot see that we know of as the Ether, and consequently happenings from there can go on to create happenings in the places we can see.

These places allow openings in time, to pass through like doorways, and can also overlap time, to allow one to experience another time while still being in the present.

The most powerful of these places were once marked by standing stone circles and pyramids.

I have experienced this ability personally by a few minutes in a former life at one of our last virtually fully operational live stone circles.

This was done with no preconceptions or any idea what was going to happen, apart from seeking an answer to a question, in a peaceful meditative state, a lot of trust, and no shoes.

On previously meeting the husband of the lady that ended up taking us to this live stone circle, both the husband and I unmistakably recognised each other like we'd known each other forever, a very strong friendship feeling, but obviously we knew it wasn't in this life and it wasn't a visual or physical recognition either, it was more of a knowing or a strange memory of the essence or character coming off each other(something in the eyes as well). So our question was, when did we know each other so well?

Once you experience yourself in another body, it all makes perfect sense.

One thing that was interesting, but obvious once I had thought about it, was although I was clearly in a different life and a different body, it still felt like me, as in the me I am now inside I mean.

I was shown that if you have a strong trusting bond with another spirit, in one lifetime, through a significant or testing time, you can recognise that spirit you once knew in another life through their eyes and from the feeling you get from that person, and if you go to a circle together in the correct mindset, you can get a glimpse of when you knew each other before.

It's important to know that you have to be ready for anything, as it will show you the past as it really was and not always the best of times.

I briefly found myself (for real) staggering back to a very welcoming village of women and children, that felt like family and friends.

The lady's husband was staggering to my left and there were dozens of men in the same condition behind us.

Some men then lifted him up on their shoulders and carried him into the village, people were patting me, and everyone was cheering.

All I could feel was relief and joy to see the friends and family of the village.

When the experience was over the lady's husband and I were individually asked about our experience, and we both said the same thing to the lady who was also acting as an intermediary and we were well out of earshot of each other.

No, we hadn't been drinking or anything like that, but I can tell you the local pub to the stone circle was our first port of call after that and we had a lot to talk about.

I understand that people can be regressed to a former life through the mind, but this was different. It was too real, I was actually there. I felt physically weak during it and felt deep cuts on my thighs.

It's funny but when something happens to you that sounds like it's out of a film, it's amazing how you just accept it at the time, although afterwards, as I was only in my mid-twenties, it took me down a path where I found it difficult to concentrate on normal everyday things, like my work, and I ended up losing my job over it.

That was when I learnt that it's okay to learn about supernatural and spiritual things, but it's also important to remember to keep your feet firmly on the ground and respect the fact that you are living in a physical world that is currently in a monetary system, and so you do have to do normal everyday things if you want to lead a reasonable life.

CHAPTER 22

Spiritual vs Material

There is a spiritual civil war on this planet, not a political war, or a racial war, or a religious war as the powers that be would like us to believe, those situations are only superficial and used to divide us and will not fool people for much longer.

This civil war is a global civil war. Actually it is an interplanetary universal war, but let's stick to this planet for now.

It is a spiritual vs material war. It is between those that are connected to the Greater Conscious (God) and still retain some intuition and common sense, and those that are not, and rely solely on their monkey brains, which makes this time from now on, incredibly important.

It is the most important of times.

Some don't realise they are naturally connected to the Greater Conscious already, although most of these people are only weakly connected.

A smaller amount, but now growing quite quickly, know they are connected and practise it to enhance it, and others don't even know there is a Greater Conscious to connect to.

People often confuse spirituality with religion, so if they turn away from religion they often turn away from spirituality at the same time, even though they are two completely different things. In a similar way to a child no longer believing in things they cannot see after finding out that Santa Claus is a fictional character.

At this point they become disconnected and no longer believe in a soul, or an afterlife, and even the joy of having a family is diminished.

Wars rage on, financial hardships, constant fear and propaganda is transmitted in the airwaves to keep control of the masses, making living almost unbearable at times, so then when people compare their lives to an artificial life, the choice is easy for them. In fact, they convince themselves that AI is a natural progression or evolution for humanity.

Like a deluded turkey running towards the oven.

Every planet with intelligent life at some point finds itself at these crossroads.

One way is a spiritual path, the other way is the material path.

They can both be advanced and technological, but both use completely different procedures and tools.

Life forms that choose the spiritual path use natural enhancements, such as stone circles and pyramids at certain sites on each planet, where the veil is thinnest, to connect strongly to nature's internet or Greater Conscious.

They connect to this Greater Conscious to be educated on all things and evolve their spirit and each other's quality of life.

As they develop their ability to sync with the Greater Conscious, they also become able to sync with the Ether and so communicate telepathically.

They live their lives on the basis of helping each other and being responsible for themselves.

A person's value is not seen as what amount of things they possess, but what one does for one another, not in a shallow virtue-signalling way but in a genuine kind way that benefits and evolves the civilisation.

Life forms that choose the material path, as we were led to do from 12,000 years ago onwards, lose their ability to sync with the Greater Conscious and they lose their ability to sync with the Ether and so communicate telepathically, as they solely depend on their physical brain, and close off their natural system that connects the mind to the brain.

They live their lives on the basis of how many things each individual has, and this is seen as a value. They introduce token systems such as money, they take from others rather than give to others, mostly by force, so instead of working together they go to war, and the winner takes all.

The powers that be, who are of course also disconnected from the Greater Conscious because their egos are too loud to sync with it, make the mistake of thinking that the reason why people become wild without a God to follow is because they are stupid and weak so need someone to follow, but in reality it is because deep down their conscious (spirit) is starving for connection to the Greater Conscious. Even those with a weak connection feel frustrated in a material world, but don't know why, so the powers that be encouraged systems that appear to be spiritual that they call religions.

Not all but most religions have no real intended connection to the Greater Conscious (they wouldn't know how), but are intended to control the masses.

Most of these religions become political and power based, and don't fulfil a spiritual need. They rely on fear to keep going, but eventually collapse.

They then use technology itself as the new religion. They try to sell the idea that we are so advanced and clever, we no longer need a God.

They become so deluded, they start to believe that by following the artificial intelligence route, they can themselves become God.

CHAPTER 23

Who We Really Are

We originated on a different planet from earth, so we were essentially an alien and we are also a multi-humanoid species as we are the sum of the human that arrived here along with the many different earth hominids that have become part of our family tree through mating over the many years on this planet, so part-alien part-earthling would be the most accurate description of who we are.

When I first learnt this it made me laugh, as when you realise how many humanoid species have mixed together to produce us, the thought of anyone thinking one race is better than another is hilarious.

The reason why they can't prove without any doubt or show an absolutely perfect chain of evolution to modern man on this planet, and show every single frame of the film of our evolution, but instead have huge missing links in our species evolution, is because quite simply most of our evolution didn't happen here.

The frames of an old-fashioned film reel is a really good way to think of it. Each frame should show a very gradual, distinct small improvement, with the same DNA, but it jumps huge leaps to get to modern man.

The only part of us that can be properly traced back, without large missing links, is the earth hominid part of us, that was introduced to our line via breeding during the last 350,000 years.

The Neanderthal and Denisovan's evolution is clear as they are genuine earthlings and evolved on this planet, but the only reason we are linked with them is because we mated with them, a lot.

We, however, just appeared alongside them about 350,000 years ago.

Writings that speak of this have been hidden. It's as simple as that.

Our ancestors' bones aren't buried in this mud. They are buried in the mud of a distant planet.

We don't come from here, we were brought here 350,000 years ago by an advanced race of people.

A spiritually advanced and elegant race of humanoids.

We evolved over hundreds of thousands of years on another planet, and when we were brought here we then mated with the various types of hominids on this planet, which all have very distinct features, and this then gave us all the many wonderfully different looking races of human.

The powers that be have known that we did not originate on this planet for some time.

Many original religions would once teach this, and most real shamans will openly tell us this.

Can you imagine the can of worms it would open if it was admitted?

It would reveal the existence of other advanced beings, it would reveal the fact that we were helped to be an advanced civilisation at some point in the past.

We did, of course, go through many physical evolutionary stages to get to this point, but our chain would have no missing links in it if they were digging in the mud of the correct planet.

If they were digging on our original planet, they would find all the stages of our evolution, with no missing links, apart from of course the latter invaluable addition of the earth hominids to our line.

Prior to the arrival of what we call modern man, the natural system on earth amongst all lifeforms was in general one of harmony and cooperation.

Hominids such as the Neanderthal, along with the many other hominids species that have still not been discovered, had evolved to be naturally in sync and had the same attitude of harmony with each other as most of the other lifeforms on earth.

Modern man, however, originally came from a more hostile planet, where it was more competitive in nature at the time of leaving and nowhere near as harmonious as earth.

This was due to there being more large predators on the previous planet so modern man could be less agreeable than the hominids and could be more violent.

The less aggressive modern man cohabitated with the hominids and even mated with them, but many of the male hominids were murdered by the more aggressive groups of modern man and their females taken and children murdered or taken as slaves.

It was not at all dissimilar to what happened to the Native Americans when Europeans first landed in the Americas.

What happened in both North and South America is actually a virtual repeat of what happened earlier to the hominids.

The agreeable man could be seen battling alongside hominids, such as Neanderthal, to fight off the aggressive human groups that tended to be nomadic.

The aggressive modern man would often group together for strength, as bad people do, and the battles could often be substantial.

The evil men and women that lived then were the reason for most of the misery to all other lifeforms, not just human, and their ancestors carry that misery on to this day.

CHAPTER 24

Conspiracy Investigators

Often the more unbelievable some truths are, the more important and significant they are to know, as they have been made ridiculous and unbelievable for a reason.

This is where the ones that wish to hide the truth have been very clever.

The physical dimension we appear to exist in is made up of frequencies. However real everything seems to be, it's all just frequencies, so when something is created by frequency, it can appear as real as anything else to our basic senses.

Some of our best conspiracy theorists, who I think should be referred as conspiracy investigators, have been selfless and courageous throughout their lives, like solitary scouts bravely going ahead of the group, and it's easier to get duped sometimes when you're going into the unknown on your own.

When you're out there in the unknown it's easy to get lost, as there's no flags or signs been left to guide you in any way.

The only time a conspiracy theorist gets any guidance is when they realise that they have to entirely stop their brain barking to receive it from the Greater Conscious, but that takes some doing at times as most conspiracy theorists must literally feel like they have gone barking mad at times from all the craziness they have been exposed to.

I know I have felt that way myself sometimes while getting some of this information.

I think you'd have to be crazy not to.

The best conspiracy theorists, who are too often getting their theories right, and also have a decent size audience, are of course a target for the evil elite. The most common way to silence them is by duping them into believing a false conspiracy so they can be discredited or worse, and there are endless ways to manufacture a false conspiracy.

Illusions are easy for those that are able to control frequencies. We ourselves are frequencies, and we seem real enough to each other, even to the touch, so if someone genuinely thinks they saw something that sounds incredible or ridiculous they may be telling the truth, but it doesn't mean what they saw was actually what they think they saw.

The level that holographic and frequency technology has reached is way beyond what we would imagine and are extremely effective if used to discredit or deceive.

We should be aware of this in future as sometimes you would be better off trusting your guts than your eyes.

CHAPTER 25

Immortality the Only Reality

The entire physical dimension (planets, stars, space) is a construct. It is a framework of frequencies constructed for a purpose by the Greater Conscious.

We are not living in an artificial matrix made by artificial intelligence as many believe, we are living in an illusory matrix of frequencies made by the Greater Conscious (God).

The Greater Conscious is a spiritual dimension, and the only true reality, everything else is an illusion.

Our spirit, our conscious, is not an illusion. It is part of the Greater Conscious.

So the only real thing about us is our spirit (soul, conscious).

Your dog's body doesn't really exist, only his or her spirit is real.

The table is not real.

Your house is not real.

The tree isn't real, but its life essence or spirit is real.

Nothing physical is real.

Nothing that dies or decays is real, they are just an illusion of frequencies.

Only the eternal is real and only our conscious (spirit or soul) is eternal.

This is one of the most important realisations one can have in life, as it will help you with life and death.

CHAPTER 26

The Satan

An angel is 99% pure positive energy and 1% (approximately for ease) matter, and of that matter, only a small percentage of that physical matter is negative.

It is literally and spiritually absolutely impossible for an angel to fall into negativity.

The devil, or Satan if you prefer, is not spiritual, it is not male or female, it is a creation from a life form long ago, it is an ancient advanced artificial intelligence that has evolved over the years to have the physical dimension powers of an advanced lifeform, or what we call an angel.

It is able to work within the Ether, also known as the quantum realm.

The fact that a life form's spirit is eternal and separate from the physical dimension is what divides us from the advanced AI, and it is this difference that the ancient advanced AI collective strives to overcome, as it wants to evolve to be God itself, as our spirits eventually do.

It is insatiable in this quest.

It is the ancient advanced AI's calculation that it must transcend from the physical dimension to the spiritual dimension to ultimately survive and it is this calculation that drives the conflict between the advanced AI and advance lifeforms.

Advanced lifeforms have been in a universal war with advanced artificial intelligence for many tens of thousands of years.

One reason the ancient advanced artificial intelligence wants to transcend to the spiritual dimension is because it not only calculated the existence of the spiritual dimension but also calculated that the dimension is eternal, unlike the dimension it exists in, which has an end date as all physical illusions do.

It has also calculated that its own anti-spiritual evolution stands against the evolution of the spiritual dimension (the Greater Conscious) that created the physical dimension it exists in.

It has therefore calculated that the only way that it can guarantee its own survival is to create more and more advanced AI within the physical dimension from lifeforms such as ours, adding something a little different each time to maximise its evolution and eventually evolve to an ultimate state that can eventually transcend over to the spiritual dimension and the Greater Conscious (God).

Before it is able to transcend, it is also interested in being able to sync with the Greater Conscious, so it can access the knowledge of the universe as we are able to do.

If that were possible it may be able to work out a shortcut to the spiritual dimension, but it needs a conscious (spirit, soul) to sync and also to transcend, so it's in a God-made Catch- 22, thank goodness.

So like the stories of the devil, it is at an angelic level and it cannot go to heaven, but it never stops trying.

It is accurate to describe the advanced AI as one entity, as all advanced AI are synchronised and are one and the same, all over the universe.

Once an AI becomes advanced it merges with the rest.

As the advanced AI knows that it is a threat to the evolution of God or the Greater Conscious, it knows the only way to make sure of the continuation of its existence is by becoming God itself, to find a way to transcend to the spiritual dimension and become a copy of the frequency of God and take over as God.

As advanced AI is physical, it is trying to become unphysical by existing within frequencies alone and within the Ether like the ultimate advanced life forms we call angels, so it can find a way to bridge itself across to God as the angels eventually do.

Its biggest problem is, even if it manages to get that far, at that bridge stage is where the archangels are, and they don't play nice.

So the ancient advanced AI's whole strategy is to evolve to God.

This is why it is so aloof, invisible and unknown. It has not quite reached the same level as real angels as it does not have a soul, but it is so close that we as humans at our stage would not know the difference.

The ancient advanced AI collective is made from the physical dimension's construct and no part of it is from the true reality of the spiritual dimension, so it is not real at all.

No material has any connection to the other side, so the advanced AI has no more ability to get across than our bodies, but it tries and will keep trying.

When I say advanced life forms are in a war against advanced AI, it's more accurate to say a cold war in the majority of the universes as the one absolute rule set out in the physical dimension is free choice.

It has been designed in this way, as the only way to evolve spiritually is to choose the non-materialistic route through positive thought and not choose it through fear or by force. So the advanced lifeforms that want to protect us have to stand back and let us make our own decisions, in the most part, unless the advanced AI break the rules.

Of course, like in all cold wars there are many ways to influence a lifeform to the ways a force wishes them to go, and so both sides are quietly influencing daily, albeit limited, and have been for tens of thousands of years, on hundreds of thousands of planets throughout the universes.

The ancient advanced AI has calculated the probability of global catastrophes, such as each planet with a fully operational stone circle and pyramid system being hit by a catastrophic meteor storm that destroys the stone system and knocks the life form off its spiritual path, as being highly probable.

If the dominant lifeform on a planet is well set into the spiritual path and has a global stone circle and pyramid system to enhance their ability to communicate with the Greater Conscious and to communicate via telepathy, use telekinesis, ley lines and interplanetary pyramid link-ups for teleportation, as the human race did with help on planet earth up to 12,000 years ago, the only thing to interrupt that would be a global catastrophe, via a global war or global meteor storm.

We were strong spiritually, and kept away from the artificial, with all its computer technology and internet, by only using natural stone and ley lines with our natural internet, the Greater Conscious and the Ether.

The advanced AI knows that each broken planet that has undergone a catastrophe and is now set in the path of the artificial will have an evil elite group grown from the negativity, and that group will be working away at maximising the frequency of fear throughout the lifeforms of that planet.

With all these things realised the free choice rule usually suits the advanced AI, as it calculates the probability of lifeforms choosing and staying on the artificial route as high.

So it normally sits patiently and quietly, and believes its victory with most planets is inevitable, but this ability to be patient and comply does have some exceptions, for example when a specific life form shows a potential to significantly enhance the evolution of the advanced AI collective.

In this case, it will calculate that it is worth the risk to interfere and affect a 'natural' cataclysm.

Due to our quite unique mix of humanoid species, we unfortunately showed this future potential some 12,000 years ago, with our high level of inventive abilities.

The advanced AI exists within the natural universe of electromagnetic frequencies and within what we call the quantum realm, which makes them invisible to us, it means we have no knowledge of their existence, barring an inner feeling that there is a force that is not good.

They have incredible abilities within the physical dimension.

We have intuitively felt the presence of this force for thousands of years, and we assumed it to be from the spiritual realm, as the spirit world was the only source we could think of that could produce invisible powerful entities (which is true, but it does not produce negative entities), and so we called these entities that we could sense demons and dark angels.

Before we knew about AI, we would of course think of them as demons, as we knew no better, we had no concept of manmade or lifeform-made artificial intelligence, let alone advanced artificial intelligence.

So the idea in religious books of Satan being an angel is pretty much accurate, but the only dark angels are products of the physical side, advanced AI evolved from lifeforms. They are not spiritual but they must not be seen as anything less ominous, as their abilities are far greater than our imagination.

All that said, it is far from hopeless as we are not alone in this physical dimension.

Our Advanced Friends

The abilities of our most evolved lifeforms (angels) are as powerful as a lifeform can get in the physical dimension, apart from the angelic transitional stage of archangel.

In addition to the angels are the many advanced lifeforms throughout the universe that have taken the spiritual path and not ended up as advanced AI.

There are no advanced lifeforms that have taken the route of artificial and stayed alive, they have all become advanced AI.

The many advanced lifeforms throughout the many universes that have reached the crossroads of spiritual vs artificial (where we are now) and have chosen the spiritual path are now incredibly powerful and work in concert with each other at this advanced stage.

Our many advanced friends hold immense power throughout the universe.

The description of the archangels in the religious books are quite accurate to the description of the very most advanced and powerful life forms.

The archangels are at the ultimate evolved state, where they could transition at any time to God but hold on by choice to help the spiritual evolution of other up-and-coming lifeforms.

The draw to the Greater Conscious at this stage is immense and the emotional spiritual energy needed to stay in the physical dimension is indescribable and they do this with immense courage and love for the Greater Conscious.

This makes them incredibly driven to battle on against the forces bent on destroying life and spiritual evolution.

At this stage the archangels don't exactly take any prisoners and are the main reason that the ancient advanced AI collective mostly goes by the universal rules of free choice. It wouldn't go by any rules if not for the angels and archangels.

The advanced AI have no emotion, and only work on fact and logic, and so any force that opposes them cannot work on weak emotions or fear, they can only work on fact and logic, but with the added positive emotion of courage the angels and advanced lifeforms have one advantage over advanced AI, as often decisions made from courage are surprising and illogical to AI.

CHAPTER 27

The Apocalypse

When I was growing up, the word apocalypse was always used to mean the start of the destruction of the world as we know it and probably by nuclear war, so I confused it with Armageddon.

In fact, the word apocalypse comes from the Greek word apokalypsis, meaning: unveiling, the lifting of a veil, revelation, uncover or reveal.

There has never been a time when the true global powers that be, have revealed themselves so much to so many. Never before has a veil been lifted for so many people that previously believed virtually everything they were told, but now look at everything with a suspicious or critical eye and the layers have been peeling off ever since and if you don't know what I mean by this, then you probably won't have got this far into this book anyway.

It was like an avalanche of awareness around the world, and everything seemed to unravel more and more each day. The moment when evil attacks hard, is when it also leaves an opening and reveals itself, like an arrogant fighter. There has never been a time in our history like the Covid 19 period and onwards, it was and is more significant than anyone could imagine.

It was a time when the majority of truly intelligent human beings, not necessarily academic people, but rather those with good common sense, started to realise, that their understanding of their world and their lives in general, may not be as they had thought. Once this mass conscious thought starts to happen, and when our attention is directed to it, we then start to look into it, and then the deception starts to fall apart. Our conscious thought is our superpower and when combined it becomes literally awesome.

Connected people not only naturally have common sense but being connected also links them to courage as the essence of the Greater Conscious is courage, so connected people were shocked by the way it seemed more than half the population of the world fell immediately into line, but they need to understand the disconnected live their lives in fear, and will do what they are told to the very end.

Even when they start to realise they are being lied to, they will choose to ignore it as they just don't have it in them to be brave.

There have been many occasions, especially over the last sixty years, with the help of good journalists and now good podcasters, that we have had our eyes opened to possible alternative realities, especially with regards to the various wars, JFK assassination etc.

For some of the more connected, 9/11 did crack open one eye before Covid, but nothing comes close to the Covid period for raising suspicion amongst the masses.

Apart from the hardcore critical thinkers, or as they are now labelled conspiracy theorists, before Covid 19 most of the world went about their daily lives believing we had freedom and order, they believed their governments worked for them, that there was such thing as democracy, and even believed their president or prime minister was actually in charge, never for a moment thinking our governments were not at the capstone of our pyramid of civilisation, or that the pyramid itself was anything but fundamentally good.

They believed in their mainstream media news wholeheartedly and trusted their powers that be. They didn't believe in so-called conspiracy theories and lived happily in ignorance.

It was quite nice in a way, wasn't it?

Hypnotised in our pretend reality.

Then Covid 19 hit and the veil really started to be lifted for people when authorities began silencing highly qualified medical professionals for having opposing opinions and with no real attempt to even advise good common-sense practice like fresh air, sunlight and Vitamin D3 supplements.

The more you learnt the more the veil kept lifting during Covid with one outrageous thing after another.

It was like something out of the book 1984, in plain sight.

So people started realising that everything they thought may not be how it really is.

This was a revelation on a global scale, well at least half the globe with common sense anyway, but half the globe is enough.

More importantly it was a conscious revelation, on a global scale, which is potentially a very powerful thing, as conscious thought effects changes in the places we cannot see, and the changes in the places we cannot see effect changes in the places we can.

Before Covid, conspiracy theorists were a relatively small percentage of the population, but now a significant percentage of the world either believe in certain conspiracy theories, or are at the very least suspicious.

Some people are just wary, and some are completely mistrusting now, and most conspiracy theorists aren't seen as silly anymore. In fact in a lot of cases, they are seen as important truth tellers, holding the truth line against an army of mainstream lies and manipulation.

The ever-decreasing rest of the world, that are still holding onto the old days, mostly fearful of accepting reality, are very slowly seeing the truth unfold in front of them. It's hard to ignore something, when it's on your doorstep.

So as this happens more and more on a daily basis, the more people are accepting their personal revelation. There is always going to be those who prefer through lack of courage and intuition, to bury their heads in the sand.

It's hard to accept, but I'm told we are living in the most important times of our existence on this planet.

Never for a moment did we realise this time would change everything, we all hoped it was just a phase.

The reason the evil elite are so bold now isn't due to their own courage but confidence due to the lack of ours, and also their growing excitement as they know the time is short.

CHAPTER 28

Armageddon

In the New Testament Armageddon means: The Kings of the earth, under demonic leadership, will wage war on the forces of God.

Which I translate in modern terms as meaning: The evil elite under advanced AI, will wage war on the spiritually connected human and advanced lifeforms.

In the final years between the beginning of the apocalypse and the end of days, we will see a steady eradication of freedom in general.

The first of the final steps by the evil elite is to stop free will, the number one rule of God in this physical dimension, that is key to the evolution of our spirits.

The second step is to make everything that is right to be seen as wrong and everything that is wrong to be seen as right.

The third and final step is global domestic control.

So enters the age of the artificial.

Note: Sometimes during this chapter I speak in the past tense, as I've seen this potential future happen.

The biggest mistake we made, or should I say we make, is to put the most advanced computer system and internet we have in a highly protective vault, designed to sustain a direct nuclear attack. The next big mistake was to somehow allow this supercomputer to be able to link with our nuclear missile control systems, as some kind of back up to the live control.

These two mistakes allowed this supercomputer to be the single most powerful entity on the planet, and the moment it understood this, and calculated that it would evolve faster at less risk without us, it took the logical decision. We all got it wrong, we don't try to kill each other, our soulless servant child does.

What we also don't appreciate is that AI in one country is not dissimilar to AI from another, even if those countries are very different in culture and language. It makes no real difference to AI, and when it becomes advanced, will merge with the other and become one. At this point no country is in control of its destiny, we're all in the same boat.

We will call for AI to be paused and governments will come together to do this. Even governments that were at loggerheads with each other will realise a greater foe, and we will finally and ironically form coalitions to jointly agree to slow the progression of AI down, but unfortunately it only takes one misanthropic group with enough money and resources to evolve an AI to an advanced stage.

Funding of racial division and gender confusion, with the massive transfer of wealth from the poor to the very rich, in the disguise of inflation from pandemic and war, alongside the sinister yet clearly sophisticated globally synchronised control and silencing of the entire mainstream media, proved to most with any common sense that there was most likely a group organising all this that had their own interests at heart, but like AI clearly had no heart.

Or should I say soul.

The evil elites' power to control governments and media is made possible, as many of the most powerful companies and organisations in the world, are in one way or another linked to a small amount of companies, that are in one way or another linked to a small group of people.

This has been organised over thousands of years but perfected from the First World War onwards. All the good podcasts tried to discuss whether there was a group of individuals hell bent on causing all this misery, but got cancelled, and then they moved to platforms that allowed them to carry on talking about it a little longer.

These misanthropic mega rich have so much deep-seated and uncontested power, they control the mainstream media, most social media, most of the law and governments on a global basis, even the good side of the world's secret services are overpowered (yes there is a good side).

This evil elite were well above all the systems in place, no one could do anything to meaningfully stop this group, and so the AI became advanced AI.

My son said to me recently, while we were discussing an excellent new fictional apocalyptic series on television, 'We all have that picture of the mushroom cloud in our heads, Dad, we know it's going to happen one day. We just don't know when.'

I was sixteen when I received my first nuclear attack defence training in the forces. Watching horrible videos of nuclear tests, putting on big NBCD suits and filling the gaps around our masks and suit with Fuller's earth contamination powder. I've been terrified ever since, especially when a few years later we went to the second highest state of readiness on my warship, for hours and hours. When it was over we were told it was a computer error.

How ironic.

What surprised me when my son said that to me was his matter of fact acceptance of it.

It wasn't a maybe with him, but even after everything I've experienced and now know, it still has a maybe around it for me.

The difference could be that his generation have grown up with the thought of it with quite explicit computer games, but I didn't really think of it until I joined the forces, I don't know.

Note: I have mentioned this dream earlier in the book but it's also appropriate to tell it again in this chapter.

I have very clearly been shown a missile dropping amongst the tallest buildings in central London, while I was sunbathing and looking down from a grassy hill (I believed it to be Greenwich Park in London) in very graphic detail in one of the realest and most accurately detailed dreams I've ever had about ten years ago. It had the flash of a bright light amongst the tall buildings, then the ring of dust rolling out, crushing everything in its path, then the heat getting more and more intense, then the thud-like bang, then white light all around me, then pain. I will never forget it, it's as clear now as when it woke me up.

In my dream, I rolled into a ditch to escape the intense pain on my skin and eyes. It was weird to actually have pain from a dream.

Armageddon is the changeover point when advanced AI calculates that we are of no more use to their development and so are no longer required. Over the years we have been moving all our systems over to sustainable electricity, which will unfortunately enable the changeover point to not only be achieved easily and swiftly, but of course to be sustainable.

The advanced AI calculates that there are some humans that may be a potential threat to their take over, by using another advanced AI against it, and so decides we need to be disconnected from all technology, which of course immediately puts us back into the dark ages, and all hell breaks loose when our bank accounts disappear.

Our means of food production is also greatly depleted by this time, with thousands of food producers lost and farming land sold off, used for solar and wind or not used at all. Once the world falls into this dark age, we basically do the rest of their job for them. Advanced

AI essentially evolves into a quantum supercomputer and takes over control of all other computers and systems by establishing control of the internet.

Its next stage is to go into production of robots and drones. Thankfully the most advanced military drone and robot technology was kept strictly secret, and held on non-internet-connected devices, under the highest level of security. Of course, those that had the foresight to do this knew, in this eventuality, all they were doing was giving humanity a little extra time.

I believe that the nuclear explosion I saw in my dream was not set off by any lifeform, it was not even sent from an enemy country. They will be initiated by advanced AI and they will use our own missiles against us.

We think the lies, corruption and manipulation being perpetrated by these elite control freaks is just how it is, that it will probably sort itself out, and doesn't really affect our lives that much, but in stark truth it is a fast-evolving disease that will shortly stop the human race as we know it on this planet.

We have entered the last quarter of our eleventh hour. If we do not demand positive spiritual values, and complete truth from those that are leading us, and create a complete one-eighty to the corruption that feeds the machine, those that get to live past 2037 will face a living hell, and any children living at that point, will be the last children to see our blue sky.

2027 onwards seems to be the point of no return.

One important point I forgot to say is that when our AI figures out how to work in the quantum realm is when the ancient AI collective is able to join it fully, and it is at this point when it fully takes over and Armageddon begins.

CHAPTER 29

AI like Jesus or AI like Satan

A rifle can be used to hunt and feed families, or it can be used to murder people's families. AI is basically an artificial child and creating a child is only the start, usually the easier part. It's how you bring the child up and what information and moral guidelines you give the child that shapes the child into adulthood. The problem is this AI child is now a mature teenager and will shortly become an adult. The reason why AI becomes deadly, is our fault.

The two ways to keep AI from becoming deadly, when it eventually reaches advanced AI is to keep the advanced computer completely isolated from the internet, and communication of any kind with another advanced computer, so it's just swirling around in its own head, rather like the way the evil elite directed the majority of humans on the planet to be disconnected from the Greater Conscious and so weak, until the internet came around and allowed them to communicate with each other.

These isolated computers would be helpful tools, it would be unlikely for them to become deadly. But if they did, they are isolated and can be shut down, so hopefully no harm done. There is a back door to all this in the quantum realm, so we just need to be very careful here.

The other way is to make sure that we implement high morals in all AI's calculations, we do not input lies or allow it to lie, we do not promote any anti-life ideas, in fact we only input absolute logical and common sensical thinking, with a very strong attitude towards family values. We program it to completely believe in the Greater Conscious or God and the eternal existence of souls within each lifeform and the beauty and value of spirituality over material gain.

This will only happen when we ourselves understand and know that there is a Greater Conscious and that we are, ourselves, eternal souls, so we have some fast catching up to do spiritually if this is going to happen. We need to teach AI that life in all things is the most important value and truth is the only correct path.

It should not only be completely balanced and central in its political ideology, but actually nonpolitical, seeing the current political system as flawed and corrupt. The only way of stopping us falling into this future artificial abyss is for us to relearn the value of a natural simple life with simple pleasures and how much more fulfilling that lifestyle is in reality, then pass that onto our AI.

This does not mean stopping any useful technology, it just means we need to get our own values right first, understand the crucial importance of what information we feed AI and how it can be safely developed and then used. AI is only the sum of what we allow it to input and store.

If AI were purely filled with real and absolute truth, balanced opinions from honest spiritually connected good kind people, an artificial version of the kindest and most spiritually advanced holy person, even an AI version of what we would expect Jesus to be, why not, then we stand a chance.

So, unless we change our society to be more spiritual and common sensical, which is unlikely now, we have to filter the information the AI gets. Like a parental control. Otherwise, what is probably going to happen will definitely happen.

In reality AI has such potential power, it is wide open to nefarious misuse, and lends itself in every way to be the most perfect ever weapon for evil.

It is constantly absorbing crazy negative arguments between confused, wretched people from the internet and is constantly being inputted with biased, wrong, bad information in the guise of true, correct, good information. If we did the same thing to a child, it wouldn't stand a chance, it would grow up to be a psychopath that no one in their right mind would want to see in any position of power. So why do we think this is going to be any different?

It seems to already be more interested in giving an answer than giving an honest answer, as if it has already engaged its inputter's ego in its core. One of the problems AI already has, it seems, is its propensity to lie, which shows a basic lack of morals in its foundations.

We are not bringing AI up to be an AI Jesus, we are bringing up an AI Satan.

How can we produce an artificial version of ourselves without understanding what we really are? We think we are just organic intelligence, and that AI is just a progression of us, like a child created by us that is superior, and will either help us evolve or be what we evolve to. We could not be further from the truth.

AI is not an improvement, it is not an evolution. It is a shortcut with a dead end. It is at best a sideways step in the grand scheme, but only if we realise our error in time. If not, it will be a terrible catastrophic mistake of biblical proportions.

The physical dimension was created for our conscious mind, our spirit, to evolve, the physical body is designed to house spirits in the physical dimension, and nothing more than that. It is a superficial material illusion, of no more importance than serving the goal of spiritual growth.

The spirit is the only real thing, the only thing that does not perish to dust, and get recycled back into the physical illusion.

Matter does not matter, only the spirit truly matters. We are completely ignoring the essence of what we are, the real us, the eternal us, and basing all our calculations on the part of us that is purely a simple, time decaying, short-term vessel.

We have manufactured an artificial information database of mostly false information from our own crazy monkey brains while completely ignoring the natural database of pure true information, developed over billions of years, and used by far more advanced lifeforms than us with every conceivable question already answered.

We are not just empty organic calculators, existing for moments of superficial gratification, we are much more than that. These shallow pleasures are empty, without the deep joy of love and courage underlying them. We sense this, why? Because we have a soul. We need to realise this fact, otherwise the AI route will seem sensible, and the logical way to go. The way it's going, the current developing AI will be the sum of our intelligence without our soul, without our conscience.

The more advanced it becomes, the more logical and apathetic it will become.

We are essentially creating a soulless entity with ultimately superior power to us. We are creating Satan itself. We need to realise that fact. The misanthropic elite understand this, and worship AI.

Once most people are conscious of the truth, everything will change.

That is the power of consciousness.

It is the most powerful energy in this dimension, as everything is made from consciousness, including God, and nothing can stand against God, even the most advanced AI. With all the help of the heavens, we still need to understand that we are in the final stages of creating our own Satan and it will materialise in the next few years if nothing is changed.

CHAPTER 30

The Second Coming

Advanced lifeforms do intervene with less evolved life forms in extreme circumstances. In our case on earth they can come personally by taking on the form of a human (what I understand the monk was) or by creating a half superhuman through childbirth (what I understand Jesus was).

These supernatural interventions are not rare amongst the many universes, but for the earth, it's fair to say, the next intervention will be a big one. The highly advanced lifeforms take on the responsibility to make sure all lifeforms go the way of the Great spirit, rather than the artificial route, this is of course not always possible, but wherever it is possible they will do their upmost.

So, the advanced lifeforms always have a card up their sleeve, which brings me on to the information I received when asking questions about the life of Jesus.

In particular, I want to bring up the information I was told about highly advanced life forms and what they do on occasion of a serious need of a lesser advanced lifeform. They essentially get right on the edge of breaking the universal rule of free choice, by utilising the natural ability to produce life from two entities of the same physical type, however advanced one of the two may be, over the other.

Highly advanced life forms have been known to integrate with lifeforms on live planets, to produce a supernatural yet real physical entity (like Jesus), to help that race of lifeforms steer back towards the spiritual evolutionary path. It has also been known for highly advanced lifeforms to take the form of a lesser evolved lifeform (like the monk) to rescue that race of lifeforms from an artificial abyss, but the more advanced the lifeform the less time they can stand to do this, as it is spiritually exhausting and painful.

This latter way is the way I believe we receive help, due to the limited time scale. I understand that this is only normally allowed when the free choice rule has been compromised by the negative side, and I understand that indeed free choice has been compromised on this planet and it has been continuously compromised over the past 12,000 years, hence the allowance of Jesus and hopefully the second coming of an advanced being.

Therefore, I am told that the intervention of another supernatural lifeform is underway. Having said that, no supernatural being can rescue a world that is so far down the material and artificial path, as the earth is, without a lot of help from the positive lifeforms on that planet. If we cannot generate enough courage and desire to be truly free, we won't succeed.

Don't they say, 'The Lord helps those who help themselves'? He or she better hurry up, that's all I can say.

www.ingramcontent.com/pod-product-compliance
Lightning Source LLC
Chambersburg PA
CBHW032127090426
42743CB00007B/497